People in the News

Daniel Radcliffe

Other books in the People in the News series:

David Beckham
Beyoncé
Kelly Clarkson
Hillary Clinton
Hilary Duff
Zac Efron
50 Cent
Tony Hawk
Salma Hayek
LeBron James
Angelina Jolie
Coretta Scott King
Ashton Kutcher
Tobey Maguire
John McCain
Barack Obama
Nancy Pelosi
Queen Latifah
Condoleezza Rice
J.K. Rowling
Shakira
Tupac Shakur
Ben Stiller
Hilary Swank
Justin Timberlake
Usher

People in the NEWS

Daniel Radcliffe

by Terri Dougherty

LUCENT BOOKS
A part of Gale, Cengage Learning

GALE
CENGAGE Learning™

Detroit • New York • San Francisco • New Haven, Conn • Waterville, Maine • London

GALE
CENGAGE Learning™

LIBRARY OF CONGRESS CATALOGING-IN-PUBLICATION DATA

Dougherty, Terri.
Daniel Radcliffe / by Terri Dougherty.
p. cm. — (People in the news)
Includes bibliographical references and index.
ISBN 978-1-4205-0156-8 (hardcover)
1. Radcliffe, Daniel, 1989—Juvenile literature. 2. Actors—Great Britain—Biography—Juvenile literature. I. Title.
PN2598.R27D68 2009
791.4302'8092—dc22
[B]

2009005290

Lucent Books
27500 Drake Rd
Farmington Hills MI 48331

ISBN-13: 978-1-4205-0156-8
ISBN-10: 1-4205-0156-9

Printed in the United States of America
1 2 3 4 5 6 7 13 12 11 10 09

Contents

Foreword

Fame and celebrity are alluring. People are drawn to those who walk in fame's spotlight, whether they are known for great accomplishments or for notorious deeds. The lives of the famous pique public interest and attract attention, perhaps because their experiences seem in some ways so different from, yet in other ways so similar to, our own.

Newspapers, magazines, and television regularly capitalize on this fascination with celebrity by running profiles of famous people. For example, television programs such as *Entertainment Tonight* devote all their programming to stories about entertainment and entertainers. Magazines such as *People* fill their pages with stories of the private lives of famous people. Even newspapers, newsmagazines, and television news programs frequently delve into the lives of well-known personalities. Despite the number of articles and programs, few provide more than a superficial glimpse at their subjects.

Lucent's People in the News series offers young readers a deeper look into the lives of today's newsmakers, the influences that have shaped them, and the impact they have had in their fields of endeavor and on other people's lives. The subjects of the series hail from many disciplines and walks of life. They include authors, musicians, athletes, political leaders, entertainers, entrepreneurs, and others who have made a mark on modern life and who, in many cases, will continue to do so for years to come.

These biographies are more than factual chronicles. Each book emphasizes the contributions, accomplishments, or deeds that have brought fame or notoriety to the individual and shows how that person has influenced modern life. Authors portray their subjects in a realistic, unsentimental light. For example, Bill Gates—the cofounder and chief executive officer of the software giant Microsoft—has been instrumental in making personal computers the most vital tool of the modern age. Few dispute his business savvy, his perseverance, or his technical expertise, yet critics say he is ruthless in his dealings with competitors, and he driven more by his desire to maintain Microsoft's dominance in the computer industry than by an interest in furthering technology.

In these books, young readers will encounter inspiring stories about real people who achieved success despite enormous obstacles. Oprah Winfrey—the most powerful, most watched, and wealthiest woman on television today—spent the first six years of her life in the care of her grandparents while her unwed mother sought work and a better life elsewhere. Her adolescence was colored by promiscuity, pregnancy at age fourteen, rape, and sexual abuse.

Each author documents and supports his or her work with an array of primary and secondary source quotations taken from diaries, letters, speeches, and interviews. All quotes are footnoted to show readers exactly how and where biographers obtained their information and provide guidance for further research. The quotations enliven the text by giving readers eyewitness views of the life and accomplishments of each person covered in the People in the News series.

In addition, each book in the series includes photographs, an annotated bibliography, a time line, and a comprehensive index. For both the casual reader and the student researcher, the People in the News series offers insight into the lives of today's newsmakers—people who shape the way we live, work, and play in the modern age.

One Role Launches a Career

When people imagine the face of Harry Potter, they see Daniel Radcliffe. Radcliffe gained instant fame when he was chosen at age eleven to take on the role of the popular boy wizard in *Harry Potter and the Sorcerer's Stone*, the first in a series of movies based on the immensely popular book series. Harry, hero of seven books by J.K. Rowling, has been a huge part of Radcliffe's preteen and teenage years, and Radcliffe's challenge has been to embrace the character without letting it consume him. Radcliffe owes his fame to Harry, but has also had to figure out how to steer his career away from the boy wizard in order to be seen as an individual and an actor rather than Harry Potter.

Being chosen to play Harry Potter was an event that shaped Radcliffe's life. Making the movies consumed a good deal of his time. Rather than attending school or playing sports, Radcliffe has been making movies. He was tutored on the sets of the Harry Potter movies, and although he missed out on school dances and activities, he never resented the hours he devoted to bringing Harry to life. He has enjoyed the challenge of taking Harry from child to adult and showing him maturing as he overcomes obstacles and fights evil.

While playing Harry, Radcliffe has grown up as well. He has gone from an inexperienced child actor to an experienced and confident adult. In his first appearance in *Harry Potter and the Sorcerer's Stone*, the eleven-year-old simply followed the directions of the movie's director. By the time the sixth

Entering the film industry as a child, Radcliffe's determination to learn and grow as an actor has brought him much success in a variety of film roles.

movie, *Harry Potter and the Half-Blood Prince*, was made, the eighteen-year-old was skilled enough to bring out layers of Harry's emotions and improvise his reactions.

Harry Potter is not the only role that has turned Radcliffe into an experienced actor. After making a few of the Potter films, he was certain he wanted to pursue a career in acting. He knew that he risked being typecast as Harry Potter if he only played that role, so he looked for opportunities to play characters with personalities that were very different from Harry's.

Radcliffe did not want to be thought of as an actor who only appeared in fantasy movies or movies for children. He chose to play a risk-taking Australian teen in the movie *December Boys*, and a young man sent off to war in the movie *My Boy Jack*. His performances in the films were met with good reviews. This was due in part to his determination not to become an egotistical child star. He did not approach his other roles as a star who wanted everyone else to follow his lead. Instead, he came in as a young actor eager to learn.

Radcliffe does not have to devote so much time to work. He earned millions working in the Potter movies, and he could simply live on the money he made from the films. However, he wants to do more with his life and does not let his wealth cloud his ambitions. He decided that he wanted to spend his time improving as an actor rather than living as an unemployed rich kid.

Radcliffe's parents helped him to have such a refreshingly mature view of his future. Alan Radcliffe and Marcia Gresham both worked in the entertainment industry and knew what stardom and ego could do to a person. Radcliffe was determined not to become like the self-indulgent actors he heard his parents talking about.

Radcliffe carefully chose his career path and made surprising and challenging choices. As a seventeen-year-old, he took on a role in the play *Equus* that not only called for him to act in front of a live audience but also required him to be naked onstage. He received stellar reviews, successfully making the move from movies to the stage.

While the role of Harry Potter gave Radcliffe the opportunity to become an actor and made him one of the wealthiest teens in the world, it also had the potential to lock him into that one role for life. However, Radcliffe's determination to learn and grow as an actor has instead allowed him to use Harry as a springboard to a career that he enjoys. He has found playing Harry to be interesting, challenging, and enjoyable and plans to play him until the movie series ends. But when the movies about Harry come to an end, it will only be the beginning for Radcliffe as an actor.

Chapter 1

A Child Eager to Act

Daniel Jacob Radcliffe was born on July 23, 1989, to Alan Radcliffe and Marcia Gresham. An only child, he grew up in Fulham, England. Fulham is in a suburb of London and part of the borough of Hammersmith and Fulham, which is home to about 175,000 people.

The entertainment industry is prominent in Fulham. It houses the television production offices of England's major broadcasting network, the British Broadcasting Corporation (BBC). Daniel's mother was a casting agent for the BBC and a casting director for British shows and movies, such as *The Inspector Lynley Mysteries* and *The Government Inspector*. Daniel's father had studied acting at the Guilford School of Acting and was an actor before becoming a literary agent.

Like many children, Daniel had his first taste of acting in a school play. Around the age of five, he had the role of a dancing monkey in a school production. He enjoyed being onstage and begged his parents to let him audition for roles in television shows and movies, but his parents were not enthusiastic about their son's desire to act. They knew what the professional acting business involved and did not want their son to be part of that business at such a young age.

While they discouraged his professional acting ambitions, his parents did not keep Daniel away from the theater. His parents enjoyed going to the theater, and took their son with them when they went to see plays. London is home to dozens of theaters,

Radcliffe at the New York premiere of his first Potter *film,* Harry Potter and the Sorcerer's Stone *in 2001.*

and the Radcliffes took advantage of the rich variety of productions the city had to offer. They did not limit their son to plays for children, but also took him to plays for adults, such as the award-winning musical *Chicago*.

Troubles in the Classroom

The theater was a place that Daniel enjoyed, but school was not. He struggled with his schoolwork at the private school he attended and was discouraged and frustrated by how challenging it was for him. One reason school was difficult was that Daniel had a mild form of developmental dyspraxia, a condition often associated with clumsiness. In Daniel's case, the condition made it difficult for him to learn things, such as how to tie his shoes. He also had a hard time with handwriting. Daniel did not excel in any subject, and when he was older, he recalled that he was "rubbish at everything at school."[1]

Daniel's parents hated to see their son struggling in school. It hurt them to see his self-confidence dwindle as he tried in vain to succeed in the classroom. Daniel had continued to ask to

Getting Recognition

When he was young, Daniel was not often singled out at school. His name was rarely mentioned during school assemblies. When he got the part as Harry Potter, however, an announcement was made that he had gotten the role. This was only the third time he had been mentioned during a school assembly. The first was when he had misbehaved, and the second was for doing well in a sports game. It may have been only the third time he was recognized at a school assembly, but thanks to the role of Harry Potter his name and face would soon be known worldwide.

be allowed to audition for professional roles, and his parents finally agreed. They wanted their son to have a chance to be successful at something and hoped that acting would give him the sense of accomplishment that was eluding him in school.

First Professional Role

Daniel had his eye on a role in a television production of Charles Dickens's *Oliver Twist*. The part had already been cast when his parents asked about an audition, but a family friend who was an acting agent suggested that Daniel audition for a part in a TV movie based on a Dickens story. The producers of *David Copperfield* were looking for an actor to play the young Copperfield. Daniel was eager to try out for the part, and his parents gave him their support. Daniel proved that he had a flair for acting and was selected for the title role.

Daniel's first acting role had him bring to life one of the most well-known characters in British literature. Set in the mid-1800s, *David Copperfield* tells the story of a young boy who is sent away to London by his stepfather after his mother dies. He encounters both misery and kindness as he struggles to survive in London, encountering a number of colorful characters along the way.

David Copperfield was released on television in Great Britain in 1999 and in the United States in spring 2000. Directed by Simon Curtis, the movie was a well-received retelling of Dickens's classic story, and several cast members' performances were nominated for awards by the British Academy of Film and Television Arts. One actress was nominated for an American award. Maggie Smith, who plays Betsey Trotwood, Copperfield's aunt, was nominated for an Emmy Award for her performance. The production captured the essence of Dickens's nine-hundred-page book, reviewer Celia Wren said, even though some details had to be left out. "Characters may have been pruned, and episodes shuffled or retouched for dramatic effect, but David Copperfield's soul is still there,"[2] Wren wrote. Although actors playing the supporting roles received most of the recognition, Terry Kelleher noted in *People* magazine that Radcliffe played Copperfield as a "quietly plucky young boy."[3]

Daniel's first acting role had him bring to life one of the most well-known characters in British literature, David Copperfield.

The Tailor of Panama

Daniel was only eleven years old, but already had a highly acclaimed acting credit. His parents allowed him to continue to follow his interest in acting, and he next got a small role in the spy film *The Tailor of Panama*. The movie, which was released in 2001, starred Pierce Brosnan and Jamie Lee Curtis and was based on a novel by John Le Carrè. Daniel played one of Curtis's children in the movie, which got four stars from movie critic Roger Ebert, who called it "a pleasure for those who like a story to unfold lovingly over a full arc."[4]

Daniel's role was not a major one, however, and his name was rarely mentioned in reviews of the film. While the movie was not a huge step in his career, it allowed him to continue acting. While he was making *The Tailor of Panama* in 2000, however, a casting call went out for child actors for another movie. This project was so big that his parents were reluctant to even tell him that auditions were under way. Plans were in place to turn author J.K. Rowling's immensely popular series of Harry Potter books into a series of movies, and the search was on for the young actors who would play the main characters.

The Search for Harry

The hunt for the young actor who would play Harry Potter was a huge undertaking. The books had a loyal following, and there was pressure to find a young actor who fit the Harry in readers' imaginations. In addition, Rowling insisted on an all-British cast, so the movie's producers had to find an actor who could satisfy both Harry's creator and his fans.

Thousands of young boys auditioned for the role of Harry Potter, yet the film's producers could not find a boy who fit the role exactly. They were looking for an actor who both looked like Harry and could convey his personality. "He had to embody so many qualities—vulnerability and strength, an inner life,"[5] producer David Heyman noted. Although the auditions did not produce the right young actor to play Harry Potter, director Christopher Columbus did find a young boy he thought was right

Not a Harry Fanatic

While Daniel liked the Harry Potter books, he admitted that he had not read as many as his classmates. By the time the first movie was made, four Potter books had been released. Daniel admitted that he was not as wild about Harry as some of his friends were. "A lot of other boys know that I've only read the first one or two books, and these boys are total fanatics," he says. "They've read all four."

Quoted in David Lott, "Daniel Radcliffe," *Daily Variety*, November 1, 2000, p. 49.

for the part. When he saw video of Daniel in *David Copperfield*, he was eager to see Daniel audition.

The film's casting director contacted Daniel's parents about having him try out for the role. If the audition was successful, the producers wanted Daniel to sign up for seven movies to be made in Los Angeles or London. Alan Radcliffe and Marcia Gresham thought over the proposal. They did not want to commit to that many films or possibly leave England. Also, they did not want their young son involved in a large project that would put so much pressure on him. They told the casting director that they did not want Daniel to try out for the role. Not wanting to disappoint their son, they did not tell him that he had been asked to audition.

After Daniel's parents told the casting director of their decision, other prospective Harry Potters were presented to Columbus as potential candidates for the role. None could compare with the image of Harry that Columbus already had in his mind, however, as his thoughts kept going back to Daniel. The casting director became so frustrated with Columbus's refusal to accept another boy that she quit, and Columbus wondered whether he would ever find the right young actor to play the important role of Harry Potter.

Director Christopher Columbus was determined to cast Radcliffe as "Harry" in the the first Potter *film.*

Fateful Theater Trip

The search for Harry continued for months without success. Then one evening, a few months before production of the first Potter film was set to begin, Daniel's parents took their son to the theater to see the play *Stones in His Pocket*. David Heyman, the principal producer of the Harry Potter movies, and Potter screenwriter Steve Kloves were also at the theater that night, sitting in the row in front of Daniel and his parents.

When Heyman and Kloves spotted Daniel with his parents, they knew they were looking at the potential star of their movie. Columbus had talked about Daniel to Heyman, and when

Heyman saw the boy in person, he realized why Columbus had been so adamant about having him audition for the role. "It was his eyes"[6] explained Heyman. Daniel's eyes made him the perfect Potter.

Heyman knew Daniel's father, and struck up a conversation with him during intermission. The next day, Heyman called Alan Radcliffe to see if he would consider allowing Daniel to audition. The chance meeting with Heyman at the theater, combined with Columbus's insistence that Daniel was right for the role, convinced his parents that Daniel should have the chance to try out for the role of Harry Potter. Daniel and his father went to lunch at the studio with Heyman and Kloves, and Daniel got to see the sets they were building for the movie. After Daniel talked to Heyman and Kloves at lunch, they asked him to come back for an audition.

The Role of a Lifetime

Daniel's parents had initially been reluctant to let him try out for the role, but Daniel needed no convincing. He was eager to audition for the part, although he became nervous when the time came to go before movie's director and producer. The character was so well-known that Daniel found the audition nerve-racking. "Even though I have been to auditions before ... this (film) is such a big thing, and the books are so successful," he said. "It was really scary."[7]

If Daniel's nervousness showed, it did not keep Columbus from wanting Daniel to play the role. Daniel did three screen tests, but the director said he knew that eleven-year-old Daniel was right for the part even before he began his audition. "Dan walked into the room and we all knew we had found Harry,"[8] Columbus said.

Daniel was not told that he already had the role. After the third screen test, he and his family returned home while the director and producer talked things over. The next day, Daniel was in the bathtub at home when his family got the telephone call informing them that Daniel had won the role. He was so happy that he cried. That night, he went to bed thinking about playing Harry Potter and

J. K. Rowling, author of the Harry Potter *series, thought Radcliffe was perfect for the lead role.*

Just a Little Like Harry

After he got the part of Harry Potter, Daniel Radcliffe was asked if he thought he was like the character he would play. His reply showed that he had a sense of humor. "I think I'm a tiny bit like Harry, 'cos I'd like to have an owl," he said. "Yeah, that's the tiny bit, actually."

Quoted in *Newsweek*, "International Perspectives," *Newsweek*, September 4, 2000, p. 19.

woke up in the middle of the night wondering if it had all been a dream. He went to his parents' room at 2 A.M. to ask if it truly was real, and they assured him it was.

The producers of the movie were not the only ones who thought Daniel was the perfect young actor to play Harry Potter. Once the selection of Daniel was announced, author J.K. Rowling gave him her seal of approval. "Having seen Dan Radcliffe's screen test, I don't think Chris Columbus could have found a better Harry,"[9] Rowling said. The announcement that Daniel would be playing Harry was made after he made *The Tailor of Panama*, and his onscreen mom in that movie also commented that he was the right choice. "The first time I laid eyes on this kid, I said, 'He's Harry Potter,'" actress Jamie Lee Curtis said. "He's the perfect choice."[10]

Getting Ready to Film

A few details had to be worked out before Daniel could put on his wizard's cloak and begin filming *Harry Potter and the Sorcerer's Stone*. The movie studio originally asked the Radcliffes to sign a contract for Daniel to appear in all seven planned Potter movies. They agreed only to the first two films, however, because they wanted to see how things went before committing to more. The Radcliffes were happy to learn that the studio had decided to film the movies in London and other locations in the England rather than in the United States.

The Radcliffes realized that the role of Harry Potter would be a life-changing one for their son and took a number of steps to make sure that the experience would be a positive one. To make sure Daniel was not pushed too hard, they talked with Columbus about protecting their son from the pressure that the role would bring. They also took steps to protect Daniel financially and set up a company called Gilmore Jacobs to handle their son's earnings from the movies. To help the family handle Daniel's acting schedule, Alan Radcliffe left his job as a literary agent to become his son's full-time chaperone.

Columbus also worked to make sure that Daniel and the other young actors in the film were not overwhelmed by the attention the movie would bring them. When Columbus directed the movie *Home Alone*, he had worked with child star Macaulay Culkin, who had family problems after becoming famous and wealthy. Columbus wanted to protect his new young stars from a similar fate. When it was time to show the world who would play Harry Potter, a press conference was set up to introduce Daniel and the other young stars. This would give fans a chance to see who would be playing the popular characters without putting too much pressure on the young actors.

The announcement that Daniel had won the role was made in August 2000, and filming was set to begin in October. The eleven-year-old was on his way to making a movie that would be part of his life for years to come. "He's got a good support system," said director John Boorman from *The Tailor of Panama*. "If anyone can withstand [the pressures] it's this boy."[11]

Bringing Harry Potter to Life

Daniel was thrilled to be chosen to play the lead role in *Harry Potter and the Sorcerer's Stone*. After the tension of auditioning and the excitement of being chosen, the real work began when he reported to the set to begin rehearsing and filming. Daniel had a big job ahead of him as he brought the world's most famous wizard to life, and his excitement over getting the role turned to dedication as he worked to get the part right.

Daniel and the rest of the movie's cast and crew had to live up to high expectations for the first Potter movie. The book series had a huge fan base, and readers all had their own ideas about how the characters would look and act. The movie had a budget of $125 million, but was expected to earn much more when it was released. It was up to Daniel and the rest of the cast to pull off a film that would satisfy the books' many fans and justify its multimillion-dollar budget.

Getting to Work

Before filming began, Daniel prepared himself for the role. He would have to do some stunts in the film, and he began learning gymnastics to get in shape for these scenes. There were also rehearsals as Daniel began going over his lines in the movie.

Daniel had more acting experience than most of the other children in the film. The other two main child characters, Rupert

"Harry" and his Snowy Owl Hedwig, who delivered messages for the young wizard.

Grint, who plays Ron, and Emma Watson, who plays Hermoine, had only acted in school plays before being cast in *Sorcerer's Stone*. The movie also had a large number of extras and young actors in smaller roles. Part of the job of director Christopher Columbus was to get the many children used to working on a movie. "The biggest challenge was the first two weeks," Columbus said. "Most of the kids were virtually unknown and had never spent time on a film set."[12] Columbus had to get the children used to working in front of a camera and not overacting as they had tended to do when performing onstage at school.

Despite his previous professional acting experience, Daniel was nervous as filming began. During rehearsals there had been fewer than a dozen people in the room. However, during filming as many as 150 extras were on the set with him. He soon learned to concentrate on what he was doing rather than be concerned with the others on the set.

Keeping His Ego in Check

During the filming of the first Harry Potter movie, Daniel Radcliffe tried not to let his ego get the best of him. He talked to his best friend, a Harry Potter fanatic, each night and told him which scenes had been filmed. However, he tried not to let the fact that he was playing Harry go to his head. "I think I've succeeded in that, and I'm proud I'm still me," he said. "My parents didn't give me any advice, so much as just being there. They are amazing: so good, so supportive. They've just been with me every step of the way." His parents were both in the entertainment business, and he heard them talk about egotistical actors. He was determined not to become one himself.

Quoted in Bonnie Churchill, "Welcome to Daniel Radcliffe's World," *Christian Science Monitor*, November 16, 2001, p. 17.

Becoming Harry

The plot of the movie stuck closely to Rowling's book, *Harry Potter and the Sorcerer's Stone*. Columbus did not want to veer from the popular story line that has eleven-year-old Harry learning he is a wizard; that his parents were killed by an evil wizard named Voldemort, not in a car accident as his aunt and uncle told him; and that he is a hero in the magical world because he had survived Voldemort's spell. Harry is whisked away to the Hogwarts School of Witchcraft and Wizardry, where he finds adventure and danger as well as friendship.

The book became popular first in England and then in the United States, and by the time the first movie was being made, there were already several books in the Potter series. Columbus did not want to change Harry, but wanted to bring the beloved character to life. "It was a very simple logical theory: if the books are so popular, why would you change them?"[13] Columbus said.

This meant that Daniel had to react to things exactly as Harry did and make sure his expressions stayed true to his character.

Not every character from the first book is in the first movie, as the plot had to be streamlined somewhat to fit it into a two-hour film. However, many details of the magical world that Harry inhabited are included, as Columbus, the cast, and the crew brought a realistic look to the picture. "Instead of trying to overtake the readers' imagination, we've just given them the best possible version of the book, which means steeping it in reality … I wanted kids to feel that if they actually took that train, Hogwarts would be waiting for them,"[14] Columbus said.

Learning Movie Magic

Many of the beautiful scenes in the movie, such as the sparkling ceiling of Hogwarts and the owls swooping in to bring students their mail, were added later, using special effects. That meant Daniel and the other actors had to react to things that were not really there. Daniel and Rupert, who played Harry's friend Ron, had to look determined as well as nervous while they played a game of magical chess on a giant board with chess pieces that exploded around them. Daniel also had to appear as he if he was flying through the air above the Quidditch field, a scene that required him to put his gymnastics training to use as he tumbled around.

One scene that did not require Daniel's imagination was one in which he encountered a 9-foot (2.7m) wall of flames in the Chamber of Secrets. The flames were real and extremely hot. Daniel had to run toward them and stop just two steps away.

Director Christopher Columbus was determined to keep the plot of the movie close to that of Rowling's book, which had a following of very devoted fans.

However, Daniel said that the most difficult scene did not involve stunts or flames. It was when Harry looked into the Mirror of Erised, which shows a person what they most desire. Harry desperately wants to have parents like his friends do, and Daniel had to figure out how to show through his expression how Harry aches to be part of a loving family. The family image was added to the mirror later with special effects, so when he was actually filming the scene, Daniel could see nothing there. "It was hard to imagine Harry's parents being there,"[15] Daniel commented.

On the Set

Daniel took his role seriously and tried his best to convey his character's emotions. He was not a skilled actor, but he listened to the director and showed the expression that the director asked him to. If Daniel had to show Harry reacting to something that would be added later with special effects, Columbus would describe to Daniel what Harry was seeing and tell Daniel how to create the right expression.

Daniel and the other children in the movie needed to be concerned with more than learning their lines and getting into character, however. They also had to attend school. Because they spent so much time on the movie set at Leavesden Studios near

Still a Regular Kid

Daniel's parents made sure that he was not treated differently because he was a celebrity. They did not let him get out of doing chores at home. There was nothing magical about his duties at home. He still had to make his bed and keep his room clean.

Radcliffe and his costars Emma Watson and Rupert Grint, who played Harry's friends and fellow students at Hogwarts.

London, they did not go to classes at a regular school but were taught by tutors in a classroom on the set for three hours each day. Since there were so many child actors who needed to fit both schoolwork and acting into their days, it took longer to make *Sorcerer's Stone* than a typical feature film.

In between schoolwork and acting, Daniel also found time for fun. He got along well with his young costars and had a good time making the movie. "If we hadn't gotten on so well, we'd have been arguing all the time," he said. "It wouldn't have been as much fun as it has been."[16] The others on the set found that Daniel could be quite the practical joker. One day, he asked a makeup lady to make it look like he had a black eye so he could shock his friends. He also played a few tricks on Robbie Coltrane, who plays Hagrid, the groundskeeper. He programmed Coltrane's phone to speak in Turkish and hid a frog in one of his boots.

Anticipation and Excitement

Daniel spent much of fall 2000 and part of early 2001 making the movie, and when his scenes were finally finished, Columbus said he was impressed with how Daniel handled the role. The young actor had been expected to bring many different qualities to the character he was playing, and managed to pull it off. "He holds the film together," Columbus said. "He's in almost every frame. Dan is an 11-year-old with a 35-year-old heart. There [is] so much depth, so much going on behind his eyes, you realize: This is a kid who has lived a life. This is a kid who can appear haunted and troubled by his past. Yet he's charming. That kind of maturity is hard to find in an 11-year-old."[17] Actor Richard Harris, who plays Dumbledore, said that all three of the main actors handled themselves well and did not let their inexperience show. "They had superb confidence in themselves,"[18] he said.

There was a great deal of anticipation over how Daniel and the others would fare on the big screen when the movie premiered in November 2001. It was first shown in London, at Odeon Leicester Square movie theater. The night before the movie's release, Daniel was so excited that he could not sleep. He woke up at several times during the night, thinking about seeing the finished movie for the first time.

The showing of the film drew a crowd filled with fans of the Potter books and many stars. Author J.K. Rowling was there, and Daniel was amazed at all the excitement surrounding the movie. "It's surreal," he said. "I've been using this word a lot recently, but it's just … surreal."[19] There were so many people taking photos at the premiere that it took Daniel's breath away and he was afraid he would pass out. He managed to keep his composure, however, and made it into the theater. All of the excitement surrounding the film made him feel numb, he said, but he was going to try and enjoy it all.

Positive Reception

The many Harry Potter fans who flocked to the movie quickly made it a financial success. It brought in more than $90 million in its opening weekend and became the top movie of 2001,

The movie's large fan base made* Harry Potter and the Sorcerer's Stone *the top movie of 2001.

bringing in more than $300 million. The movie's budget of $125 million was more than justified given such impressive box office returns.

While the fans loved seeing their beloved book characters onscreen, critics were not wild about Columbus's decision to stay true to the book. The movie had "many charms, but few surprises,"[20] noted reviewer Lisa Schwarzbaum. Reviewer Leah Rozen said the film was more interesting for children than adults. Although she enjoyed the film's beginning, she said it lost its magic as it dragged on and turned into more of an adventure film. "The breathless sense of determination and discovery that characterizes Harry's early scenes vanishes partway through the movie, which runs a foot-jiggling 2 hours and 22 minutes, when Harry and his wizard pals begin making like junior action heroes and battling evil,"[21] Rozen said.

Most reviewers said Daniel was the right choice for the role, although his acting was not applauded by everyone. Writer Stanley Kauffmann said Daniel did not bring anything special to the role, commenting that "Daniel Radcliffe is an unexceptional boy in every way."[22] However, many reviewers said Daniel accurately captured Harry's personality. Reviewer David Ansen said that the casting of Daniel and his costars was one of the film's successes and Schwarzbaum said Daniel's portrayal of Harry blended well with his costars, and noted that, "Radcliffe's mature self-possession, his soft handsomeness and unfussy sweetness as Harry play off the Our Gang gung-ho spirit of ginger-headed Rupert Grint as classmate Ron Weasley."[23]

Making *Chamber of Secrets*

Harry Potter and the Sorcerer's Stone was a hit, but there was little time for Daniel to relax and bask in the success of the first movie. Soon it was time to work on the second movie, *Harry Potter and the Chamber of Secrets*. Preparation for the second film had begun even before the first movie was released, so it could be ready for theaters in November 2002.

In* Chamber of Secrets, *Hogwarts students are threatened by an evil force lurking within the walls of the school.

In *Harry Potter and the Chamber of Secrets*, Harry faces more monsters, including giant spiders and a huge snake, as well as Lord Voldemort. The plot includes action and danger, as Hogwarts students are threatened by an evil force lurking within the walls of the school. There are lighter moments as well, as Harry and Ron head to Hogwarts in a flying car and encounter a clueless defense against the dark arts teacher, Gilderoy Lockhart, played by Kenneth Branagh.

Although Branagh was new to the cast, much about the making of the second movie was familiar for Daniel. It was no surprise that he, Rupert, and Emma once again played the three main characters; they had agreed to do the second film at the same time they had signed on for the first one. Columbus again directed the movie and, for his second turn as Harry, Daniel felt very at ease with the director. He was more confident in his acting, and mentioned his ideas to Columbus if he thought a scene should be played in a particular way. Columbus saw that

Daniel had improved as an actor. "Dan's an incredibly bright, serious person, and he has taken the time to work on his craft day after day for two years, so he's really become much more professional,"[24] he said.

Daniel was more self-assured about his acting in the second movie, but he still had to pick up new skills for the role. He had to learn a bit about fencing for a dueling wand scene that ended up needing dozens of takes before the actors were finished. Harry also speaks in the language of Parseltongue, a language invented by Rowling that was spoken by snakes, and Daniel had to appear to be communicating in the unusual language.

As he thought more about his role, Daniel came to realize that he was much like the character he played. When he first got the role of Harry, he had commented that the only way he was like Harry was that they both liked owls. Now it was almost scary for him to think about how much he and Harry had in common. "I think I'm going to have to have therapy one day. When I read the Potter books, I find out more things about myself that Harry has in his personality too," he said. "We have curiosity, loyalty and get in trouble. We don't break the rules, we just kind of bend them."[25]

Life as a Movie Star

Like the character he played, Daniel had also become a popular figure. His face was on Harry Potter merchandise, from toys and video games to paper towels. It was odd for him to see himself as a celebrity. "The oddest thing was seeing myself as a Lego action figure," he said. "It was so strange seeing my cylindrical head."[26]

Life as Harry Potter, however, was not always fun. After the first movie came out, things changed for Daniel at the private school he attended when he was not on the movie set. He returned to his regular classes when he was not working and was picked on by other kids. Because he was a celebrity, some kids thought it would be fun to bully him. "Some people did get very aggressive," he said. "People say it was just jealously, but I don't think it was jealously. I think it's just 'We can have a crack at the kid that plays Harry Potter.'"[27]

His parents tried to keep Daniel's life as stable as possible. However, his day-to-day life was different than that of an average teen. There was always the chance that he would be recognized when he was out in public. One time when a girl screamed after recognizing him, he was so shocked that he screamed back.

Although it was sometimes awkward to be noticed by fans, Daniel did enjoy some of the perks that came with being a celebrity. He said the best part was meeting movie stars. At the London premiere of *Secrets*, he met actor Ben Stiller, and at the New York premier he met actors Tim Robbins and Susan Sarandon.

Fans Love *Chamber of Secrets*

Daniel was treated like a celebrity himself by the fans who turned out for the premiere of the second Harry Potter film in November

Entertaining the Cast and Crew

It was exciting for Daniel and the others working on the movie *Harry Potter and the Chamber of Secrets* to be part of another Harry Potter movie, but making the film was not always fun. There was a great deal of boring downtime. Daniel helped alleviate some of the boredom between takes. "A lot of fooling about happens behind takes," noted Emma Watson, who plays Hermoine. "We had a week with 300 extras in the Great Hall, it's boiling hot, the food stinks, everyone is dying of boredom, and we have to make everybody laugh. It got so bad that Dan had to get up onto the table with Robbie Coltrane [who plays groundskeeper Hagrid] and dance. He did the cancan. He did the Macarena. The whole hall was laughing."

Quoted in Daniel Fierman, "Harry Potter and the Challenge of Sequels," *Entertainment Weekly*, November 22, 2002, p. 24.

Teenage fans loved Radcliffe so much they would chant his name at premieres and other public appearances. The young actor found it both "strange" and "exciting."

2002. Teen girls chanted his name before the first showing of the movie in London, and Daniel took it in stride. "It is really strange, but very exciting,"[28] he said.

As they had with *Sorcerer's Stone*, fans made *Harry Potter and the Chamber of Secrets* a financial success. The movie brought in $88 million during its opening weekend as families turned out to see Harry take on Lord Voldemort a second time. Critics liked it more than *Sorcerer's Stone*, but saw it as a movie for kids rather than adults. Reviewer Leah Rozen compared Harry to a young Indiana Jones as he fights against spiders and enormous snakes. While the young actors did a fine job, Rozen said that there is so much action that the characters' personalities do not have a chance to develop. Reviewer Mike Clark, however, liked the action and quicker pace of the movie. He applauded Columbus for not following Rowling's book as rigorously as he had with the first movie. Clark said that the second film has more whimsy and spirit than the first. He also applauded Daniel's performance. "Radcliffe as Harry seems more assured. Now in his second year at Hogwarts and teetering on the cusp of his teenage years, Harry, too, is more comfortable with his wizardly status,"[29] Clark said.

Other reviewers also noticed that Daniel seemed more confident in his role as Harry. Lisa Schwarzbaum said that Daniel was blossoming into a "charming and handsome young man," and added that the three main actors were developing a good rapport. "The contrasting personalities and acting styles of young Daniel Radcliffe, Rupert Grint, and Emma Watson as Harry and his wizard-in-training schoolmates Ron Weasley and Hermione Granger blend into a complementary group pluckiness,"[30] she said.

No Doubt He Is Harry

After the success of the second film, it was certain that Daniel would continue to play Harry Potter for at least one more film. He had shown that he had the talent and work ethic to handle the part, and he had become synonymous with his character in the hearts of fans. He was not outgrowing the role, although his voice was deepening and he was getting taller as he matured. "In the books, the kids get progressively older at Hogwarts, so they could presumably play their roles for the seven films," Columbus noted. "It's really up to them."[31]

Daniel had improved as an actor over the course of the first two films, but for the most part he had played it safe as he carefully followed the director's instructions. He had not wanted to risk ruining the movies that would be so important to fans of the book, and his approach worked as fans helped the films earn nearly $1 billion. He received praise for his work and kept a level head as stardom descended upon him. The filmmaking process did not overwhelm him, as his parents had initially feared it would when they reluctantly agreed to let him audition for the role. Instead, he thrived on it and looked forward to continuing to play Harry.

Chapter 3

Daniel and Harry Grow Up

Daniel's character was growing up and so was he. Both Harry and Daniel were now teenagers and as Harry's personality matured and the challenges he faced grew more complex. Daniel had to show Harry's feelings toward love and revenge, as well as danger and adventure.

Daniel continued to enjoy the role of Harry Potter, but he was not the same actor he had been when the series began. Experience was making him more polished as he learned how to channel his emotions and display them onscreen more adeptly. He needed to deliver deeper performances as the character he was playing was becoming more demanding as the movie series went on. Changes that were occurring on the set of the movie would help him meet the challenge his character presented.

The Director Departs

Daniel, as well as Rupert Grint as Ron and Emma Watson as Hermoine, stayed on for the third film. There were changes behind the scenes, however, that brought some differences to the set of *Harry Potter and the Prisoner of Azkaban*. Director Christopher Columbus announced that he was too exhausted to continue directing the Potter movies and that he wanted to spend more time with his family. He stayed on as a producer of the third film, so he could still have some oversight of the

Christopher Columbus decided not to direct the third film, Harry Potter and the Prisoner of Azkaban, *but stayed on as producer.*

Quiddich Challenge

One of the most difficult scenes for Daniel Radcliffe to film in *Prisoner of Azkaban* was the Quiddich tournament sequence. The game, which has the players flying on broomsticks and trying to catch a flying ball called a snitch, was supposed to take place in a cold rainstorm. To make it look like he was playing in a downpour Daniel had to be hosed down before each take. To make it a little more comfortable for him, warm rather than cold water was used during the soggy scene.

As the cameras rolled, more water fell on him. Although he had been uncomfortable while doing the action-packed scene, when he saw the finished result, he felt his efforts were worth it. "It just looks brilliant!" he said.

Quoted in Sean Smith and Devin Gordon, "Daniel Radcliffe; *Harry Potter and the Prisoner of Azkaban*," *Newsweek*, May 10, 2004, p. 54.

project and offer advice to the next director, but a new person would be giving Daniel, Rupert, and Emma direction on how to play their roles.

It was not easy for the young actors to say good-bye to Columbus. He had not only cared about their work onscreen, but had also been interested in them as people and had tried to protect them from the pressures and difficulties that can arise for child actors. Daniel felt horrible after Columbus told him that he would not be back for the third movie. Columbus had taught him a great deal about acting and movies, and it was difficult for Daniel to imagine someone else in the director's chair.

Daniel was unsure of what to expect from a new director, but he believed that Columbus was leaving the third movie and the young actors in good hands. "Chris would never let anything bad happen to us, I trust him," Daniel said. "It's Chris Columbus' legacy and I think he found someone who would carry it on."[32]

Cuaron Takes the Director's Chair

Daniel had a good attitude about the change in directors, but it was still not easy to get used to someone new. New director Alfonso Cuaron had worked with children before in movies, such as *A Little Princess*, but he had a different style of working with young actors than Columbus did. He asked more of the children in the movie as he encouraged them to get inside their characters' minds.

One way Cuaron helped Daniel and the others prepare for their roles in *Prisoner of Azkaban* was by having them write an essay about the character they played. Daniel was not wild about this at first. "I thought, 'Who is this man, coming in here and giving us homework?' "[33] he said. Although he wrote only one page about Harry, Daniel eventually came to see that the essay was a good exercise. As he wrote about Harry's mindset in *Azkaban*, he brought out ideas of Harry being arrogant and angry as he became a teen. As he talked his thoughts over with the director, it helped them set the tone for Harry's attitude in the film.

Star Treatment

Before *Prisoner of Azkaban* was released, Daniel and the rest of the cast had to do television and magazine interviews to generate publicity for it. Daniel admitted that he was still not used to being thought of as a star. While he appreciated the attention, he did not want to ever start thinking it was normal. "It always still fazes me. The moment I stop being kind of surprised by it or overwhelmed, is a really bad moment, 'cause you know, it's a really strange thing getting out of a car, and there are all these people screaming," he said. "But it's amazing, it really is."

Quoted in Sean Smith and Devin Gordon, "Daniel Radcliffe; *Harry Potter and the Prisoner of Azkaban*," *Newsweek*, May 10, 2004, p. 54.

Another way Cuaron helped Daniel capture Harry's personality as he moved from childhood to adolescence was by having him watch movies that were about children who were coping with the challenges that the teen years bring. In films such as *The Bicycle Thief*, Daniel saw characters working through the loss of childhood. This helped him understand what Harry was going through and how he should portray his feelings in the movie.

Playing a Troubled Harry

Although he had played Harry to positive reviews in two movies already, Daniel had to change the way he approached the character in the third film. Harry was changing, and Daniel's performance needed to reflect that. In *Prisoner of Azkaban*, Harry is a thirteen-year-old who wants more independence and control over his life. He becomes frustrated with the aunt and uncle who mistreat him and is ready to strike out on his own. He learns he has a godfather, Sirius Black, a killer who has escaped from the Azkaban prison. He also has his first encounter with Dementors, which suck the soul out of their victims and are especially keen on tormenting Harry. There is concern that Harry will be killed, but he wants to take his protection into his own hands rather rely on others. He also must cope with a desire to get revenge for the deaths of his parents.

Daniel had quite a bit to learn about displaying emotion as he prepared for his scenes as Harry. He also had to get used to Cuaron's style of filming for longer periods of time than Columbus had. Because the scenes were longer, it forced the young actors to get more of their lines and their actions right on the first try. It required patience on the part of Daniel and the others as they worked to do things to the director's liking. For some scenes, it took as long as two weeks for Daniel and everyone to get things exactly right.

Especially difficult for Daniel was a scene in which he vowed to kill Sirius Black. He wanted to get the emotion just right, but Cuaron would not tell him how to do it. Instead, the director helped him figure out the scene and let Daniel come up with the right

In Harry Potter and the Prisoner of Azkaban, *not only does Harry come into adolescence but Radcliffe as well.*

expression by himself. Daniel listened to music to help get in the right mood and just before the scene was filmed he thought about his dog that had died a few years before. Although it was more difficult for him to conjure his own emotions than to have the director tell him how to look or act in the scene, he was happy to do it this way. Figuring things out for himself taught him more about acting and made him better at it. "I'll forever be in his debt," Daniel said. "It basically affected the way I approached everything after that."[34]

Cuaron Takes a Chance

Changing how the child actors handled their parts was not the only change Cuaron made for the third movie. Unlike Columbus, who had remained true to the details of the books in his movies, Cuaron changed a few things. Hermoine was given a more heroic role, and information about Harry's Firebolt broomstick was moved from the beginning of the story to the end.

It was risky to make changes to such a well-known story. But although the first two movies had done well at the box office, they had not been hits with critics. Cuaron was looking to make a film that was a good movie on its own merits, not just a retelling of a story that only appealed to fans of the book.

The movie needed to show how Harry was maturing and how the way he looked at the world was changing as he tried to take more control over his life. Very early in the movie, Daniel needed to show that Harry was growing up. When a pompous aunt continually criticizes his parents, Harry's anger flares, and he performs a spell that inflates the woman like a balloon. In the earlier movies, Daniel displays a childlike innocence and wonder as Harry learns he was a wizard. In this film, Daniel had to show anger and frustration as Harry yearns for more independence.

Audiences and Critics Approve

The work that Daniel and the others put into improving their acting abilities and the darker look of the film paid off. *Harry Potter and the Prisoner of Azkaban* was hailed as a success by both critics

Gary Oldman joined the cast of **Prisoner of Azkaban** *as Harry's godfather Sirius Black.*

and fans. Movie critic Ty Burr liked the way the movie combined the real-life theme of a child turning into a teen with the imaginative world of wizards. "*Azkaban* is nicely balanced between high-flying fantasy (the Hippogriff; a particularly rough game of Quidditch) and growing adolescent rebellion, and between the charming ordinariness of leads Radcliffe, Watson, and Rupert Grint and the skill of heavyweights Gary Oldman, David Thewlis, and Emma Thompson,"[35] Burr said.

No Illusions

Daniel gets positive reviews for his work as Harry Potter and is a well-known figure around the world. Yet he maintains a modest view of himself. When he was complimented on his physique for a bathtub scene in *Harry Potter and the Goblet of Fire,* he admitted he was not smooth when it came to talking to girls. "Guys my age, they think they're suave, but they're rubbish and they know it," the sixteen-year-old said.

Although he is a star himself, that does not keep him from becoming tongue-tied around people he admires. When members of the band Radiohead appeared in *Goblet of Fire's* Yule Ball scene, Daniel admitted that he was too nervous and awestruck to talk to them when they were on the set.

He is also honest about his musical ability. He enjoys playing bass guitar, but is realistic about the idea of becoming a rock star. "The future of music doesn't rest on me," he said. "If I formed a band, I don't think anyone would say, 'Wow! What was he doing acting?' "

Quoted in Jeff Jensen, "Daniel Radcliffe," *Entertainment Weekly,* November 11, 2005, p. 26.

Along with the changes in Harry came a change in the movie's audience. While the first two films had been aimed at a younger audience, this one appealed more to older children and adults because of its dark tone and emotions. "Unlike earlier Potter films, where you often felt as if you were watching kids ape grown-up action heroes, the emphasis here is on an adolescent Harry and his pals meeting dangerous challenges with measured courage and ingenuity rather than just derring-do,"[36] reviewer Leah Rozen said.

Daniel had worked hard to make Harry's changing attitude evident in the film, and critics noticed that his acting skills were improving. The emotions he showed Harry experiencing came from inside himself and were not just the result of a director telling him what to do. "The kid has turned into an actor,"[37] said reviewer Steve Vineberg. Sean Smith of *Newsweek* noted that Daniel's performance was "far more impressive this time around."[38]

New Tastes, Abilities, and Interests

Like Harry, Daniel was growing up and developing new interests. His admiration for the World Wrestling Federation was fading, and he had developed a taste for more sophisticated movies while making *Prisoner of Akzaban*. These films included *12 Angry Men*, a classic movie about a jury deciding whether to convict an accused killer, and director Wes Anderson's dry comedy *The Royal Tenenbaums*.

Daniel's taste in music was also evolving. He liked listening to the classic punk rock of the Sex Pistols, the New York Dolls, and the Stranglers. He was also learning to play bass guitar. Actor Gary Oldman, who plays Harry's godfather, Sirius Black, had worked with Daniel while they were on the set of *Prisoner of Azkaban* and taught him to play "Come Together" by the Beatles. Daniel enjoyed playing so much that he had thoughts of starting a band one day.

Although he had developed a love for music, acting was still Daniel's favorite pastime. He liked playing Harry Potter and wanted to continue playing him as long as he could. Harry was an interesting character, Daniel noted, because of his imperfections. "I like playing someone who is a complete under-dog. Harry is a huge hero, but he's not perfect," Daniel said. "He's completely awkward around girls. He's not a perfect student. He just scrapes by."[39]

Growing Up as Harry

Bringing Harry to life onscreen had been a huge undertaking for Daniel. Playing the world's most famous wizard in a series of extremely successful films had changed his life immensely, but with three Potter films to his credit, Daniel was not fazed by the

Radcliffe's love for music increased as he got older. Here, he attends a Red Hot Chili Peppers concert at Hyde Park in London, 2004.

increased attention and fame the role brought. "I've got quite a surreal mind anyway, so I don't think it's made much difference to how I see everything," he said. "That's what's weird: I don't think of it as being that bizarre."[40]

Daniel did not let stardom change him. When it came time to do interviews to promote the movies, he was very relaxed around reporters and even showed one writer that he could belly dance. The teenager had a quick wit and gave clever replies to questions. When asked about dealing with the changes that adolescence brings, he said, "I'm just going through what every other teenager goes through, but with posters."[41]

Although acting meant that Daniel's life revolved around shooting schedules and movie releases, he did not mind working and going to school on the set. Being tutored on the set also meant that he could not participate in sports or other typical school activities, but he preferred juggling schoolwork and acting to being in a regular school full time. "There's never been a day when I've thought I really don't want to be here," he said about his time on the set. "Because for me, it's this or school. And I've never really loved being in school that much."[42]

Preparations for *Goblet of Fire*

Daniel's easygoing nature and love of acting helped him adapt to more changes on the set of the next Potter film. Cuaron was praised for the changes and the rich look he brought to the third Potter film, but he had known from the beginning he would only be directing one movie in the series. Directing the Harry Potter movies was demanding and time-consuming, and he wanted to do only one before moving on to another project.

The fourth movie, *Harry Potter and the Goblet of Fire*, would be directed by Mike Newell. The British director had done movies for adults, such as *Four Weddings and a Funeral* and the thriller *Donnie Brasco* with Al Pacino and Johnny Depp. He had also directed episodes of the television program *The Young Indiana Jones Chronicles*. He was an experienced director who knew how to give heavy material a light touch.

Friends, But Not BFFs

While making *Harry Potter and the Goblet of Fire*, fifteen-year-old Daniel got along well with his costars, but was not especially close to them. In the movies, Harry and Ron are best friends, in real life Rupert Grint is several years older than Daniel and like Daniel had his own circle of friends. "Rupert I don't know that well," Daniel commented. "I think it's partly because he finished school before I did." He was better friends with Emma Watson, who was closer to his age, but there was nothing romantic about their relationship. "I had a big crush on her when I first met her, definitely," he says. "But she's more like a sister now."

Quoted in Lev Grossman, "Growing Up Potter," *Time*, November 7, 2005, p. 113.

Harry Potter and the Goblet of Fire has its share of dark and scary moments as well as sensitive and humorous ones. Harry and his friends deal with the terrifying prospect of Lord Voldemort returning but are also consumed with typical teenage concerns such as wondering how to ask a girl to a dance. The plot of the movie centers around Harry preparing for and completing a trio of dangerous tasks in the Tri-Wizard Tournament and dealing with friction with friends who are jealous and suspicious of his motives. In addition to the puzzling and dangerous tournament challenges, he also copes with realistic nightmares involving Voldemort.

The role called for Daniel to continue to add layers of emotional complexity to his character. He had to show the uncertainty and unease that a teen often feels when talking to a member of the opposite sex, and as well as fear and hatred when facing Lord Voldemort. In addition, there was shock and anguish over the death of a friend. Some of the issues were so weighty that Daniel commented that it did not seem like he was playing a kid in the movie.

Giving *Goblet* His All

Daniel worked on showing Harry's deepening emotions in the fourth film. In addition, he prepared and trained for some physically demanding scenes. In one scene, which had Harry being chased by a dragon, he had to fall down a roof. It was terrifying for him to fall so far and fast while filming the scene, but he did what was required of him in order to make the movie the best it could be.

An underwater scene was also challenging. He trained for six months to perfect his swimming skills, so Harry could dive in and swim underwater to rescue a friend. He got two ear infections along the way, but was happy he was able to do the scene without the help of a double, a stuntman who does dangerous or physically difficult scenes in place of the actor. He knew the completed scene would look better with him doing it. "There was talk of someone else doing it and superimposing my face on it," he said. "That would have looked like rubbish."[43]

Daniel was determined to work hard to make the film a success. He did a better job of focusing his energy than he had when he

For* Goblet of Fire, *Daniel had to work harder to express his emotions and perform more demanding physical tasks.

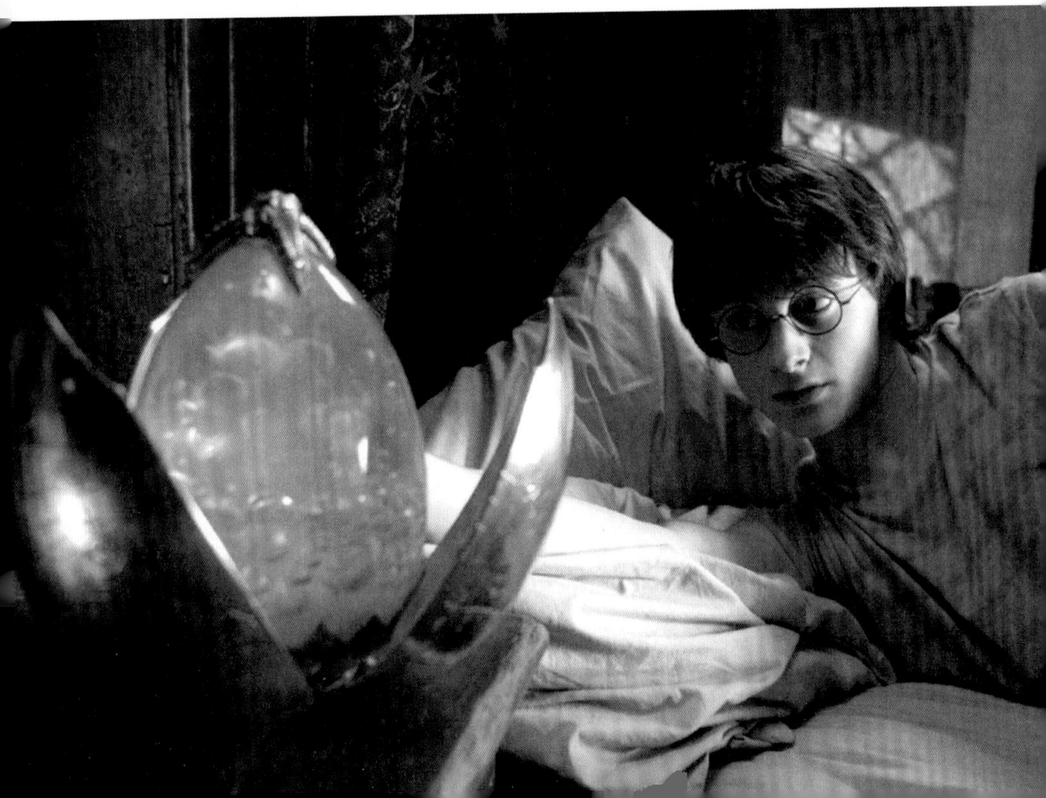

was younger. He was more self-assured about playing Harry and more comfortable with offering suggestions about his character, even if his ideas were not always heeded. "I'm finding it's better to say something than not say anything,"[44] he commented.

Although he was improving, Daniel did not get overconfident about his acting ability. He did not want to come across as egotistical or as a difficult child star. Newell said he enjoyed working with Daniel, who was assured in his role but not cocky. Daniel seemed comfortable with the role, but at the same time was not complacent; he knew he still had a great deal to learn when it came to acting.

Rewarding Reviews

When the reviews for *Harry Potter and the Goblet of Fire* came out, it was apparent that Daniel had learned his lessons well. The movie was released in December 2005, and critics were impressed. "This one does deserve mega-hit status," said Shirley Sealy. "The action in *Goblet of Fire* is more exalting and faster-paced than in previous Potter films, and visually, it is by far the most splendid."[45] The movie was praised for combining danger, humor, and the emotions that go along with being a teenager. The cast was getting looser, reviewer Peter Travers noted in *Rolling Stone* magazine, and he called the movie "hard to resist."[46] Fans gave their approval as well, and the film was a commercial success. It earned $102 million in one weekend and took in more money overall than *Prisoner of Azkaban* had.

Although the movie received a good deal of fan support and critical praise, not everyone was pleased with the tone of the film. Reviewer Owen Gleiberman liked the strong performances by the movie's supporting characters, such as Brendan Gleeson as Mad-Eye Moody and Maggie Smith as Professor McGonagall, but said that the film lacked the emotion of the previous movie. "Newell, unlike Cuaron, jams sequences together like bricks of LEGO, without giving the story emotional flow,"[47] Gleiberman said.

Although some critics wanted the movie to emphasize the character's feelings and emotions more deeply, the performances

Harry Potter and the Goblet of Fire *was released in 2005. Critics described it as "splendid" and the film grossed more money than* **Prisoner of Azkaban.**

of the young actors received praise. "It is now apparent that [Daniel] and his onscreen buddies Grint and Watson are turning into accomplished young actors,"[48] *People* magazine noted. Steve Kloves, the screenwriter for the Potter movies, said the three young stars were responsible for the growing popularity of the Potter movies because fans returned to the theater to see how their old friends were growing up. "People are fascinated with seeing them grow up and change," he said. "They are the heartbeat of the franchise."[49]

Growing as an Actor

Each time he took on the character of Harry Potter, Daniel found something new to present in his performance. He enjoyed the process of acting and made a point to soak in information from his fellow actors. He had learned to successfully adapt to the styles of new directors. With every movie and every new director he worked with, he learned something more about how to approach his role. "I might as well be playing a different person each film, because he changes so much,"[50] Daniel noted.

Throughout all the changes, Daniel remained committed to his role. He also developed a love for acting itself, and while he wanted to continue to play Harry, he also wanted to grow as an actor. To do this, he decided to take some time between the fourth and fifth Potter movies to step into a new role. He wanted to try a smaller role in a movie that would let him stretch his acting ability. He knew he ultimately learned and grew from all the new people he worked with, and he wanted to become a better actor and not just be the boy who played Harry Potter.

Chapter 4

A Career beyond Harry

Although he was only sixteen and committed to making three more movies in the Harry Potter series, Daniel was already thinking about his career beyond the role of the young wizard. Although Harry changed significantly in each movie, and Daniel felt he was playing an entirely different character in each film, to moviegoers he was Harry Potter. As wonderful as the role was, Daniel did not want to get typecast as the young wizard, and he began searching for a different role to take on during breaks in filming the Potter series.

Daniel was often asked if he feared being typecast as Harry, and while he did not think that would happen, he decided to take steps sooner rather than later in order to prevent it. "It would make a lot more sense to start doing different things before [the] *Harry Potter* [films] ended, sort of in conjunction with them, rather than waiting till they're all done and then trying to break away,"[51] he said.

Working Down Under

Daniel's first opportunity to take a different role came in late 2005. After the release of the fourth Potter film, Daniel traveled to Australia to make the movie *December Boys*. The movie was vastly different than the Harry Potter franchise. It had a much smaller budget and a lesser-known cast of actors. It was based on a book by Michael Noonan, which was popular in Australia but had nowhere near the worldwide readership of the Harry Potter books.

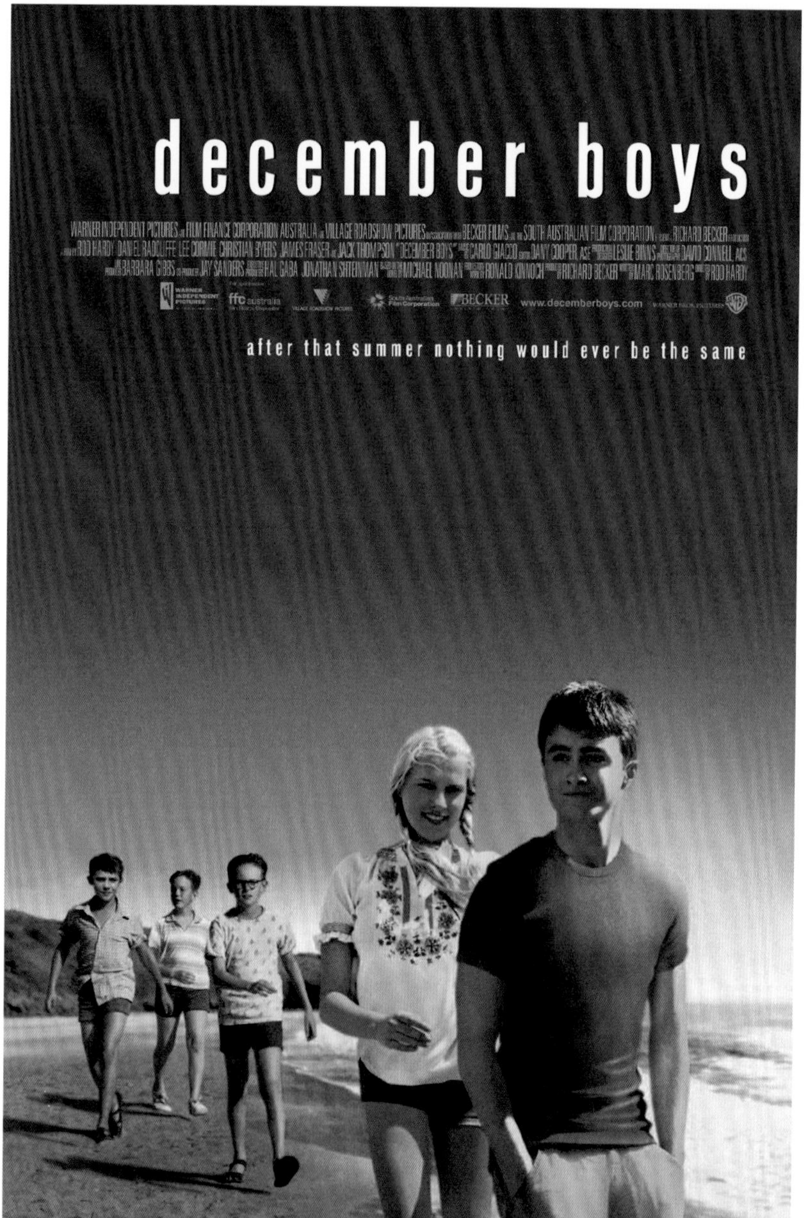

Daniel did not want to get typecast as the young wizard, and he began searching for a different role to take on during breaks in filming the Potter series, such as December Boys.

Although it did not have the makings of a blockbuster, *December Boys* was a good choice for Daniel at this stage in his career. It was a role he could learn something from without being scrutinized heavily. This smaller role in a little-known film was the perfect place for him to test his ability as an actor.

Becoming Maps

Daniel's character in *December Boys* is Maps, an Australian orphan. The character is nothing like Harry Potter. Maps is a responsible child at school but during a seaside vacation, a rebellious side emerges and he drinks and smokes. He also has a romantic relationship with a girl he meets while on vacation.

The movie is set in southern Australia in the early 1960s. Maps and three other orphans who have December birthdays are chosen to take a vacation on the beach. The boys have a wonderful time staying with a retired naval officer and his wife, but become edgy when they learn that a French woman and her husband who are also on vacation may be making plans to adopt one of them. Daniel's character is a leader and the oldest of the four boys, and at 17 thinks he is too old to be adopted. The story takes another turn when Maps meets a girl and falls in love for the first time.

The story focuses on family, friendship, and young love, and Daniel liked the emotions the script evoked. He hoped he had the ability to bring those emotions across onscreen. It would be a test of his acting ability to see if he could step into a new role and have audiences see Maps rather than Harry Potter.

New Places and New Faces

In addition to stepping into a new character, Daniel had to work with a completely different cast and crew for the first time since stepping into the role of Harry Potter. He would also be working with another new director. *December Boys* would be directed by Rod Hardy, whose previous work included directing television shows such as *X-Files* and *JAG*.

In* December Boys, *Radcliffe plays "Maps," a 17-year-old orphan who thinks he is too old to be adopted.

Before filming began in Australia, Daniel was nervous about how he would be accepted on the set. He was the most well-known of the cast members and did not want to be seen as an egotistical child star. He was unsure how the cast and crew would react to him and wondered what they expected him to be like.

Daniel's easygoing and hardworking personality helped him fit in right away. He was eagerly accepted by the cast and crew when it became clear that he would not be demanding or egotistical. "Luckily, I'm not that person, so they were very, very accepting of me," he said. "Because I wasn't being horrible and throwing things."[52]

As Daniel worked with a new cast and crew and became more comfortable with his new role, he gained confidence in himself as an actor. He saw that he could get into character as Maps and give him a distinct personality. Even though *December Boys* was not a film with a huge budget or a long list of stars, Daniel took the role of Maps just as seriously as he did Harry Potter. He wanted to show that he could successfully play someone other than the famous boy wizard. "I just needed to prove to myself that I could absolutely go off and do something else,"[53] he said.

Praise for Daniel

Daniel's chance to show moviegoers that he could be someone other than Harry Potter came when *December Boys* was released in Australia in 2006 and the United States in 2007. While he got good reviews for his work in the film, the movie itself generated little fanfare. Unlike the Potter movies, it was not eagerly anticipated and did not generate a great deal of publicity before it was shown in theaters. The film did not receive critical acclaim or bring crowds of people to the box office.

Critics and moviegoers in the United States both met the movie with a shrug. It was released in few U.S. theaters, and the story was criticized for being unoriginal and dull. Reviewer Russell Edwards noted that all of the young actors, except for Daniel, could have used a director who was firmer with them. If not for Daniel's star power, the movie probably would not have been released outside Australia. "It's nothing you haven't seen a dozen or more times before," movie critic David Noh said. "Which one of the boys will find a happy home is the big mystery of the plot, but, such is the film's lack of originality, you don't really care much."[54]

While some critics liked the movie's nostalgic feel, the story did not evoke the emotions in the audience that Daniel had hoped it would. However, the movie did show that he could do a good job of playing someone other than Harry Potter. Daniel had taken a chance with this role, and he earned respect for successfully stepping into a new character. Film critic Lisa Schwarzbaum said his maturity and experience were evident in the movie, and Noh applauded his acting ability. "It's nice news to report that, devoid of horn rims, he really can act, and does so with a graceful modesty that is careful not to too easily upstage his less experienced, younger costars,"[55] Noh said. The film also drew a large audience outside of the United States, and while it did not make the millions of the Harry Potter films, it did end up bringing in more than $1 million worldwide.

A More Mature Harry

The skills Daniel learned working on *December Boys* would be needed when he was called upon to deliver a performance as a more

For** **Harry Potter and the Order of the Phoenix,** **Radcliffe played a darker, more serious role that required him to express a variety of intense emotions.

thoughtful, serious, and angry Harry in the next Potter film, *Harry Potter and the Order of the Phoenix*. The role of Harry was becoming more complex, and Daniel's acting needed to be up to the challenge. In order to bring out the changes in Harry, Daniel spent a great deal of time learning how to convey Harry's heightened emotions.

Harry Potter and the Order of the Phoenix was even darker in tone than the previous Potter films. As Harry gets close to adulthood, the world he lives in is getting closer to a battle between good and evil. Harry must cope with guilt over the death of a friend, rumors that he is lying about Voldemort's return, and a cold shoulder from his friend Dumbledore. In a lighter vein, Harry was growing into an adult and also had typical teen concerns. He is a fifteen-year-old with a serious crush on a classmate and is thinking about his first kiss.

In the fifth movie, Harry is angry and frustrated that those in authority fail to see the truth about Lord Voldemort's return. As he struggles to get others to believe in the return of Lord Voldemort, he reluctantly becomes a leader as he teaches his friends how to battle during secret defense against the dark arts lessons. He faces new opponents, such as the sweet-faced but cruel Delores Umbridge, who refuses to believe Voldemort could be back, and ultimately learns that his friends can play an important role in the fight against Voldemort. He learns to control the anger he feels and realizes that love and friendship are the things that truly matter.

A New Team

The change in Harry's demeanor and the movie's tone was once again handled by a new director, and a new screenwriter was also brought onboard. Director David Yates and screenwriter

The Right Amount of Anger

While making *Harry Potter and the Order of the Phoenix*, director David Yates had to decide how angry Harry should appear. Harry feels alone because some of his friends do not believe that Lord Voldemort has returned, and he thinks that the headmaster Dumbledore is neglecting him when he needs him most. At one point in the movie, Harry bursts out with the comment, "I just feel so angry all the time." While Yates wanted Daniel to display Harry's frustration and anger over the circumstances he was in, he also wanted Harry to remain a likable character. To do this, Daniel had to show the struggles that were behind Harry's anger. "If he got too angry, he wouldn't be very likable or sympathetic, so we trod a fine line to service the notion that someone who's troubled and conflicted and misunderstood has the right to be angry," Yates commented. "We tried to present it so you feel for his plight, so the anger is rational."

Quoted in Claudia Puig, "Dark Magic Haunts Hogwarts," *USA Today*, July 10, 2007.

A Deeper Harry

In *Harry Potter and the Order of the Phoenix,* screenwriter Michael Goldenberg was brought in to work on his first Harry Potter movie. He made Harry a more thoughtful character than Daniel had previously played. "It is a much more interior journey than the previous films," Goldenberg said. "Harry is struggling. He's haunted. He's isolated and misunderstood and has a deep longing to connect. He's so emotionally impacted that he's a coiled spring."

Goldenberg felt comfortable that fans would accept this version of Harry because they knew he was a good person. One of Goldenberg's favorite scenes has Daniel showing how Harry was trying to get Dumbledore's attention. "He's trying to catch his eye and finally just screams 'Look at me!'" Goldenberg said. "Harry is afraid of his pent-up rage that's out of control. He worries he's been damaged by all he's been through, if it's broken him, and he's become bad."

Quoted in Claudia Puig, "Dark Magic Haunts Hogwarts," *USA Today,* July 10, 2007.

Michael Goldenberg set a faster pace for this movie and assumed that the audience watching the film was already familiar with the characters. They wanted to approach the movie in a streamlined manner and spent little time onscreen introducing the characters. They cut out details about Harry's strained friendship with Ron and Hermoine, Quidditch matches, and ghosts and instead concentrated on the movie's plot and action. "Michael Goldenberg and I both clearly knew the story we wanted to tell," explained Yates. "It's about Harry and the conflicts he has about his identity, and being misunderstood. It was surprising how many things fell away when you just concentrate on the one central spine."[56]

Yates, whose previous directing experience consisted mainly of British television dramas, encouraged Daniel to add more emotion to the character than he did in previous films. He wanted Daniel to show more of Harry's inner struggles. "I was keen to make this a much more psychological, emotional Harry than we've seen before," Yates said."[57]

Ready to Be Pushed

Yates brought a new directing style to the movie as he did things his own way. Before shooting a scene, he spent a great deal of time on rehearsal, noting that, "the most important thing on screen is the actors. If the performance isn't real, that million-dollar special-effects shot behind the actor doesn't count for anything."[58] To that end, he worked with Daniel before filming began to help him give a richer performance as Harry. He saw that Daniel was up to the task. "He's a very intuitive person, very bright, quite sensitive," Yates said. "I'm just helping him wake those things up. You can see his determination and ambition, and he can switch things on a sixpence, so I can't wait for people to see what he's achieving."[59]

Daniel, who turned seventeen as the movie was being filmed near London in 2006, was eager to add nuances to his character.

Director David Yates (second from left) pushed Radcliffe's performance in* Order of the Phoenix *to new heights. Here, the group is at Grauman's Chinese Theatre at the film's U.S. premiere in 2007.

"I'm at a stage now where I'm ready to be pushed further by a director,"[60] he said. Daniel was able to take Yates's ideas and suggestions and improve his performance. "David wants everything to be real and detailed," Daniel said. "So if I'm doing, say, a quite general sense of fear, he'll come up and quietly say, 'I think you can do it better, Dan.' He'll be completely frank with me. I don't think there's been a moment on set this time where I've walked away after a scene and thought I didn't give it my all."[61]

Daniel noted that the physical challenges and stunts were more demanding in *Goblet of Fire* but that the acting was more difficult in *Order of the Phoenix*. In addition to the anger and frustration Harry felt, Daniel also had to show how Harry was nervous about his first kiss, the guilt he felt about the death of his friend Cedric Digory, and the grief he experienced upon the death of his godfather, Sirius Black. It was not easy for him to capture Harry's feelings. "Doing the real isolation and anger and hurt he feels has been a challenge," Daniel said while the movie was being made. "Thankfully, I've never been bereaved in my life so I don't know what it's like, but it is incredibly difficult to act the Sirius stuff."[62]

Connecting to Harry's Emotions

In order to portray what his character was feeling, Daniel imagined what other people in similar real-life circumstances must feel like. When he rallied his friends as they prepared to battle Lord Voldemort, he thought about the people in France who resisted the Germans who occupied their country during World War II. To help understand the grief and guilt Harry felt about the death of Cedric Digory, Daniel talked to a grief counselor. The counselor also helped Daniel understand how Cedric's death impacted Harry's relationship with Cho Chang, Cedric's girlfriend.

To accurately portray Harry, Daniel also got help from the ultimate Harry Potter expert: author J.K. Rowling. Daniel talked with Rowling for an hour about how he should portray Harry's relationship with his godfather, Sirius Black. Sirius was close friends with Harry's father, and with his parents dead, Harry looks

Radcliffe was nervous about filming "Harry's" first onscreen kiss, which was in* Order of the Phoenix. *It took thirty takes before Radcliffe and costar Katie Leung got it right.

to Sirius for guidance and a feeling of family. "She stressed the importance of Harry's relationship with Sirius," Daniel said. "It is the absolute most important relationship of his life."[63]

In addition to displaying Harry's heavy emotions, Daniel also faced the challenge of filming Harry's first kiss. Daniel had already done romantic scenes before, in *December Boys*, but this was different. Harry's first kiss was a pivotal moment in his life, and fans would be intrigued to see how he handled it. It took all day for Daniel and Katie Leung, who plays Cho Chang, to film the scene. But after thirty takes, they got it right. "Katie and I were both a bit awkward and nervous at first, but once we got into it, it was fine,"[64] he said, and Leung later commented to the press that Daniel was a good kisser.

The fifth Potter movie was a challenge to make, but after filming was finished Daniel was proud of what he had accomplished. He liked bringing out the changes in Harry and showing his deep emotions. "[The fifth film] is far and away my favorite," he said. "Harry is quite a ferocious character."[65]

A Personal Milestone

Daniel was continually reaching new goals as an actor, and while on the set of *Order of the Phoenix*, he reached a milestone in his personal life as well. During the ten-month filming shoot, he finished

Sneak Peak

Daniel did not get to see early drafts of J.K. Rowling's Potter books before they were published, but his work on the movies did give him a little bit of insight into what she had planned for the series. He made the fifth Harry Potter movie, *Harry Potter and the Order of the Phoenix*, before the final book was released and an early draft of the script did not have the house-elf Kreacher in it. Rowling let the scriptwriter know that the house-elf living at the Order of the Phoenix headquarters should be in the movie, so Daniel knew that he must play an important role later in the series. "All she said was, 'Put him back in.' So I knew very casually that he was in the seventh book," Daniel said.

Quoted in *USA Today*, "Daniel Radcliffe, Torn between Two Worlds," *USA Today*, July 2007.

his on-set schooling. He was seventeen and was no longer required to spend three hours each day on the set doing schoolwork.

By now Daniel was certain of what he wanted to do with his life and career. He wanted be a professional actor and decided not to go to college. The decision surprised some people, but he was confident about this move. "You mention to somebody that you don't want to go to university, and they look at you like you're failing your kind," he said. "I certainly don't think I'd enjoy it very much. I think I work much better educating myself." [66]

Daniel enjoys learning but never thrived in a formal educational setting. One of the ways he continued to feed his intellect was by reading. He read classics, such as books by F. Scott Fitzgerald and Emile Zola. He also dabbled with writing scripts, short stories, and poetry.

Separate from Harry

Just as he was looking to stretch himself intellectually, Daniel also wanted to continue to grow as an actor. He looked forward to a career onstage and in movies where he was known as Daniel Radcliffe, not

Harry Potter. He knew it would take some effort on his part and more than minor roles in productions such as *December Boys* to accomplish this. Some people might always see him as Harry, but that would not stop him from looking for other acting opportunities. "There probably will be some people that never quite separate me from Harry," he said. "I'm just going to get on with it."[67]

In addition to looking for roles in other movies and plays, Daniel showed the public that he was not young Harry Potter in other ways as well. He worked out to build up his muscles, and he posed shirtless for *Details* magazine. He wanted to make it clear that he was growing up and was his own person, distinctly different from the popular character he played.

Daniel was proud of his work as Harry and planned to portray him in the final films in the series. However, he felt that he needed to continue to take roles that veered away from Harry in order to establish a solid acting career. In order to broaden his acting skills, Daniel looked for challenging roles both onscreen and onstage.

Conquering the Stage

Before *Harry Potter and the Order of the Phoenix* was released, Daniel made a surprising and edgy career move. For his next acting project, he took to the stage. He auditioned for and was cast in the lead role in *Equus*, a revival of a 1970s drama. Acting in *Equus* would be vastly different than anything Daniel had done before. Not only was it a live production, but it was a role that called for him to be naked onstage for several minutes.

With this play, Daniel was taking a huge chance with his career. It could set him apart from Harry and show him to be a great actor, or it could be an embarrassing disappointment for him. There was risk and pressure involved as Daniel would be performing before a live audience each night in a role in which there were no retakes or second chances. He also risked offending people who still saw him as the young Harry Potter, not an older teen ready to take on a demanding and very different role.

Daniel looked forward to the challenge. He knew it would not be easy to make the adjustment from screen to stage, but he enjoyed learning and saw this as an opportunity to grow as an actor. If he succeeded, it would make a huge impact on his acting career.

Making the Right Choice

Daniel did not choose the play *Equus* on a whim. He thought carefully about the type of part that would best separate him from Harry Potter. He did not want to choose a character that was too much like Harry,

Radcliffe made a risky move starring in the live stage production of* Equus*. Not only was the play a success it proved Radcliffe to be a talented and diverse actor.

but he did not want to do something too wild or unusual either. He also wanted to make it clear that he was no longer a child.

In order to strike this balance, Daniel looked for a character that challenged him but did not make it seem that he was doing anything just to get away from Harry Potter. "If I went off and did another fantasy film, everyone would say, 'He's not even trying,' but if I went off and played a drug dealer, they'd say, 'God, he's trying way too hard,'"[68] Daniel said.

Daniel found what he was looking for in *Equus*. The character of Alan Strang, a mentally disturbed young man, is a serious and difficult role. It would certainly allow him to stretch his acting ability. And, by making a move to the theater instead of another movie, he would have the opportunity to learn about a different style of acting.

Theater Actor

Before *Equus*, Daniel had appeared only briefly onstage. He was in a school production when he was five years old, and his only other work onstage was in 2002, during a break in filming the Harry Potter series. It was in the comedy *The Play What I Wrote*, directed by Kenneth Branagh, who plays Gilderoy Lockhart in *Harry Potter and the Chamber of Secrets*. The play includes a scene that has the actors staging a play, and each night a special guest star made an appearance in the cast.

Daniel appeared in the spoof, playing the son of a count who must go out wearing a disguise. For the role, Daniel wore a pink dress and wig. Although he was only onstage one night, his appearance made an impression on the play's producer, David Pugh. "He had incredible presence and was very professional,"[69] Pugh said.

Impressive Audition

Daniel's small role in *The Play What I Wrote* helped him get the part in *Equus*. When it came time for Pugh to find an actor for the teen lead in *Equus*, he remembered Daniel. Late in 2005, as Daniel was looking into acting opportunities beyond Harry Potter, he heard from Pugh. He auditioned and again impressed both Pugh and the

Radcliffe with* Equus *director Thea Sharrock (center) and fellow* Equus *actor Richard Griffiths at an after party for the play in New York City.

play's author, Peter Shaffer. *Equus* had originally been produced in the 1970s, and Shaffer had been reluctant to agree to a revival unless the right person could be found to play the central role. When he saw Daniel audition, he gave Pugh permission to do the play.

Thea Sharrock was chosen as the director, and Daniel also had to prove to her that he was right for the role. When she first met with him, she was impressed by his confidence that he could take on the part. It was obvious to her that he was more than the boy who played Harry Potter; he was a disciplined actor eager to take on a new role and prove that he was up to the challenge. "When I was approached to direct [*Equus*], I said if Daniel doesn't do it for me, we should look elsewhere," she said. "But I had a very positive response from our first meeting."[70]

Security was tight as people tried to get a look at how the play's preparations were going. There were concerns when the play opened that people would come to the theater only to see Daniel take off his clothes. Sharrock emphasized that the play was about much more than that. "I just hope they [the audiences] realize that not only is the play not about nakedness, but that he really can act,"[71] she said.

Not for Money

Daniel wanted the role in *Equus* for the acting experience, not for a paycheck. There was no financial need for him to take on more work. He made $15 million in salary in 2006 and was one of Britain's richest teens. Despite his wealth, Daniel still wanted to act and take on roles that were both different and demanding. He wanted to show the world that he was no longer a child and that he was committed to his career. "With this, they can say I'm good or terrible but the one thing they can't say is I haven't challenged myself,"[72] Daniel said.

Daniel saw the role as a sort of rite of passage for him as an actor. He noted that many actors who he admired had at one time or another appeared naked onstage. He saw Alan Strang as an interesting character and the ten minutes of onstage nudity as a necessary and pivotal part of the play. Daniel did not worry too much about the nude scene, although at one point before the play opened he asked his dad if he thought he could wear pants instead of taking off his clothes. A larger concern to him was his

Dealing with the End

When the seventh and final book in the Harry Potter series was released in 2007, Daniel admitted that it was an odd feeling to have the series end. The first book had been published in Great Britain in 1998, and fans had eagerly awaited the release of each sequel. The movies were also met with great excitement and anticipation. "It's a bizarre feeling," he said. "It's absolutely the end of an era. These films have influenced a generation of kids into reading at a moment when everybody thought reading was something that was becoming less popular among kids. That is an amazing thing for somebody to have done."

Daniel was not worried that the end of the book series would hurt interest in the remaining movies in the series. Even when people knew the ending to a story, they still liked to see the film version, he reasoned. "People have always known the endings of the books and seen the movies anyway," he said. "People knew *Titanic* would not have a happy ending. And with *Apollo 13*, we knew they got back all right. But people still went to see those movies."

Quoted in *USA Today*, "Daniel Radcliffe, Torn between Two Worlds," *USA Today*, July 2007.

lack of experience in live theater, so he took acting lessons, did vocal exercises, and worked on projecting his voice.

In addition to the nude scene, there were other shocking things about the role to people who were used to seeing Daniel only as Harry Potter. In *Equus*, Daniel's character is a troubled young man who smokes and swears. He works in a stable and blinds six horses in a fit of rage. The story unfolds as a psychiatrist, played by Richard Griffiths (who plays Harry's Uncle Vernon in the *Potter* films), tries to find out what provoked his outburst.

There were some people who thought Daniel was about to damage his career by acting in the play. They predicted that playing such an unsettling character would bring his acting career crashing to a halt. Daniel, however, was determined to prove them wrong.

Radcliffe's role in Equus *not only required him to smoke onstage but to perform naked in some scenes—much different than playing "Harry."*

He was certain that he had the ability to play the role and that this was something he should be doing. "If you can do something like *Equus*, that has a much different, more grown-up audience, I think that shows people you really want to try out different things," he said. "It makes them take you more seriously."[73]

Good Reviews for Daniel

Between February and June 2007, Daniel was onstage eight times a week in *Equus*. He performed each night before a crowd of nine hundred people in the Gielgud Theatre. The show soon became the hottest one on London's West End.

Daniel received strong reviews for his portrayal of Alan Strang, although critics were not excited about the play overall. Many commented that the themes of the play were out-of-date. "Daniel Radcliffe is pretty much the whole show in a disappointing West End revival of *Equus*," reviewer Matt Wolf said. "Radcliffe brings real intensity and theatrical presence to a part that requires him to bare all, physically and emotionally."[74] Wolf added that Daniel's performance indicated that he had an acting career ahead of him, and Ray Bennett of the *Hollywood Reporter* noted that Daniel looked confident onstage.

The chance Daniel took with this role paid off. He was successful in getting people to see a new character when he took to the stage and was applauded for his efforts. Michael Gambon, who plays Dumbledore in several Potter movies, said Daniel's role helped redefine him. "He's growing up. He's a proper theater actor now,"[75] Gambon said.

Back to Harry

Daniel performed in *Equus* for sixteen weeks and then returned to the role that had made him famous. He returned to familiar territory in mid-2008 as filming began for the sixth Harry Potter movie, *Harry Potter and the Half-Blood Prince*. The fifth Potter movie, *Harry Potter and the Order of the Phoenix*, was released that summer and he was also called upon to do interviews to promote it.

Although he wanted to make sure he had a career after the Potter movies were finished, Daniel was also proud to continue to play Harry and worked hard to promote the films. For a month before *Order of the Phoenix* was released, he went on a busy month-long publicity tour for the film. His pride in his work and in the movie made it easy to talk about the film.

After performing onstage in *Equus*, Daniel admitted that he had not been sure how he would feel about watching himself onscreen as Harry Potter. He had learned so much about acting during his months onstage that he thought he might wish he had done things differently. However, he also had faith that the movie's director had coached him to do a fine performance, and when he saw the movie, he was pleased. "I actually didn't mind watching myself, for sort of the first time in five films," he said. "I have got better. Thank God! I still see a lot of room for improvement, obviously. But I've started to see Harry rather than myself."[76]

Wild about Harry

The Harry Potter that Daniel plays in *Order of the Phoenix* is a more serious, frustrated, and angrier Harry than he plays in the earlier films. The plot edges closer to the final showdown

Radcliffe returned to promoting the* Potter *films and was honored along with the cast in a Hand, Foot, and Wand-Print Ceremony at Grauman's Chinese Theatre in Hollywood, California.

What Should Happen to Harry?

Before the seventh and final book, *Harry Potter and the Deathly Hallows*, was published, Daniel was asked what he thought would happen to Harry at the end of the book. Daniel said he expected him to die at the hand of Voldemort. He said. "I think it will be quite exciting if the only way Voldemort could be killed is if Harry dies as well. There is a very strong connection between them."

Quoted in Mike Goodridge, "Harry's Welcome Back to World," *Evening Standard*, May 31, 2007.

between Harry and Lord Voldemort, as Harry works to convince people that Voldemort has returned and teaches his friends how to fight. The film has a darker tone than previous films, with an opening scene showing Harry in an empty schoolyard, indicating that his childhood is a faded memory.

The changes that director David Yates made to the plot in order to condense the story bothered some critics. A subplot involving Harry having a strained relationship with Ron and Hermoine is largely absent from the film, and some minor characters are not mentioned. Reviewer David Ansen of *Newsweek* said the movie was a letdown after the two previous films, and that Daniel had the ability to do even more with the part than he was allowed to show onscreen. "Radcliffe is clearly willing and able to take Harry to deeper, darker places, but the screenplay doesn't give him enough to play off of—his newly embattled relationships with Ron and Hermione didn't make it to the screen," he wrote. "The storytelling seems occasionally disjointed, but more important, for all the special-effects wizardry, that touch of film magic never surfaces. There's fireworks and action and much swooshing about, but this interim installment seems stuck in one nightmarish gear."[77]

Other reviewers, however, liked the film's tight storyline, its focus on action, and its more serious tone. Reviewer Leah Rozen of *People* magazine enjoyed the movie, saying, "The spell cast by these movies grows stronger with each film."[78] The movie was also a hit with fans. In the first five days of its release, it brought in almost $140 million.

No matter what they thought of the movie, reviewers were universal in their praise for Daniel. Reviewer Steve Vineberg of *Christian Century* magazine called Daniel's performance his finest so far, and Rozen noted that he continued to improve, saying. "Radcliffe continues to mature as an actor, giving Harry complex shadings."[79] Reviewer Lisa Schwarzbaum said Daniel gave a believable performance and noted that he was in good shape for the role.

In *Time* magazine, Richard Corliss agreed that Daniel had done a fine job with his character. Daniel was able to show that Harry knew a great battle lay ahead and that a great deal of its success rested on his shoulders. "Precociously wise, Harry also seems prematurely tired, a wizened wizard at 15. And Radcliffe measures up to his character; his bold shadings reveal Harry as both tortured adolescent and an epic hero ready to do battle," Corliss said. "All of which makes Potter 5 not just a ripping yarn, but a powerful, poignant coming-of-age story."[80]

Continuing as Harry

Daniel was now eighteen, two years older than the character he would be playing in the next movie, *Harry Potter and the Half-Blood Prince*. Although some people wondered if he was too mature to play the younger Harry, he did not feel he was outgrowing the part. He noted that many actors played characters that were younger than they were. "People come up to me and say, 'Do you not think you're getting too old for the part?' It's lunacy,"[81] he said.

Daniel was growing and changing, just as Harry was. Daniel learned something with each new director he worked with and got tips from the seasoned pros such as Maggie Smith, Gary Oldman, and Alan Rickman. Daniel looked forward to being part of the final films in the series.

It was sometimes questioned that Radcliffe was getting too old to play the part of "Harry," but he enjoyed growing with the character and even won a National Movie Award in 2007.

Becoming a Skilled Actor

While the end was in sight for the Potter movie franchise, Daniel made it clear that this was only the beginning of his career.

His performances in *Equus* and *December Boys* had shown that he was becoming a skilled actor who could take on demanding

Friendships

As his fame and wealth grew, it was not always easy for Daniel to know if people wanted to be his friend because they really liked him, or because he is famous. His best friend was Will Steggle, who was his dresser on the Harry Potter films. Steggle was in his forties, and was decades older than Daniel, but Daniel did not see their friendship as strange. "Mentally he's younger than me," Daniel said. "It's not really [weird] for me, because I've grown up around adults."

Daniel noted that he met most of the girls he dated through work, but added that he doubted that he would develop a serious relationship with an actress. "I think it would be very hard to go out with an actress, because they're mad," he said. "Some actresses are just insane. I've never worked with a nasty actress—they're all absolutely delightful. But completely barking [crazy]."

Quoted in Simon Garfield, "Daniel Radcliffe," *Details*, http://men.style.com/details/features/landing?id=content_5746.

roles. *Equus* was a risky move that paid off, but Daniel knew that it would take more than one appearance onstage to separate him from his well-known character. "I'll have that eternal association with Potter, which can't be solved by doing just one play," he says. "It's going to take a lot of work, but I'm willing to put that in."[82]

One person who believed that Daniel had the talent and drive to forge a long and successful career was director David Yates who had worked with Daniel on *Order of the Phoenix*. "He has an incredible work ethic, and he's determined to push himself as an actor," Yates said. "I just think he's going to get better and better. He's going to make some very smart choices because he's got quite discerning taste and he's incredibly perceptive and well-read and has good instincts."[83]

Yates watched Daniel take the Harry Potter character to new emotional depths in the fifth movie. Although the movie's style had received mixed reviews, there was no question Daniel was becoming a fine actor.

Chapter 6

Ready for Adult Roles

Daniel's reputation as a talented actor grew. He showed that he was willing challenge himself and work to improve as an actor. He continued to look for diverse roles that would set him apart from Harry Potter and move him into more adult roles. He would play Harry in the final films of the series, but breaks in the filming schedule gave him the opportunity to focus on his career.

Daniel steered his career toward thoughtful and serious dramatic parts that let him explore different characters and circumstances. He did not take parts that would make it look like he was desperate to shake off the wizard's cloak, but chose roles that provided good learning opportunities. He was rewarded for his efforts with positive reviews and the opportunity to take his acclaimed Alan Strang to Broadway.

My Boy Jack

In summer 2007, Daniel took a solemn turn away from his Harry Potter character with a role in the television movie *My Boy Jack*. The movie, set during World War I, is based on the true story of famed British author Rudyard Kipling, whose son fought with the Irish Guards against the Germans in France. Directed by Brian Kirk, the film is adapted from a 1997 stage play and takes its title from a poem by Kipling.

Some scenes from* My Boy Jack *were filmed at Rudyard Kipling's home in East Sussex, England, an experience that proved very emotional for Daniel.

Based on historical events, *My Boy Jack* is very different from the Harry Potter films. There are no fantastical or magical elements in the drama that deals with a young man's duty to his country and a family's grief. The film looks at a father's expectations for his son, a son's desire for independence, and the tragedy of war.

In the film, Kipling is an avid supporter of Britain's war effort during World War I and helps his son get into the army. His son has terrible eyesight and would not have been required to serve in the military. However, Kipling wants his son to be a soldier and is proud to see him have the chance to experience what he perceives as the glory of war.

While Kipling admires his son for fulfilling his duty to his country, his son is more interested in joining the army in order to get away from the confines of his home. However, the experience is nothing like either father or son imagined it would be. Jack becomes

Close to Family

Throughout the Harry Potter films and other acting work, Daniel continued to live in the house where he grew up in Fulham, England. He continued to get along well with his parents, who came with him to New York when he starred in *Equus* there. They support him and make sure he keeps his perspective about his work. "Sometimes I can feel a bit sorry for myself if I've been lying down in the mud for the night shoot and then I have to get up at 4:30 the next morning," he said. "But my mum and dad have always said, if anyone's complaining, 'Well, you're not down a mine.'"

"Actors give themselves a bad reputation, and I think it's a shame," he added. "It's why some people resent them for being famous and think they do no work comparatively. But it's a great job. And it's not down a mine."

Quoted in Sarah Lyall, "Onstage, Stripped of that Wizardry," *New York Times*, September 14, 2008.

a leader in the Irish Guards and embroiled in terrible trench warfare in northern France. He must cope with the rain and mud in the trenches and is killed on the first day of battle.

Learning Experience

The role called for Daniel to portray the teenage Jack and show him maturing as he takes on the challenge of army life. As Jack learns from his experiences, he grows and becomes a leader of his men. Tragically, he must lead them over the top of the trenches in France to their death.

The part pushed Daniel as an actor and also taught him about history and what it would have been like to be growing up at such a difficult time. "It's a heartbreaking but beautifully told story," he said. "History can sometimes feel like a list of acts.

It becomes interesting to me when you can envisage what an individual might have been thinking at the time of a momentous event."[84]

While making the movie, Daniel got a feel for what Jack's life had been like. The scene in which Jack leaves for war was filmed at the Kipling home in East Sussex, England. Being at the home where Jack lived was an emotional experience for Daniel. "Every time I walked out of the house, I could see out of the corner of my eye a stone in the arch where Jack had carved his initials," Daniel said. "It was really moving."[85]

Solid Performance

My Boy Jack was shown in England in 2007 on Remembrance Sunday, a holiday celebrated in November each year that is similar to America's Veterans Day. Daniel's performance as a teen coping with such daunting circumstances was praised. "Taking his first crack at playing an adult, Daniel Radcliffe scores a minor triumph as Rudyard Kipling's 18-year-old son who marched off to the front soon after the outbreak of World War I and quickly disappeared in the mud and waste of the killing fields,"[86] reviewer Laurence Vittes wrote in the *Hollywood Reporter–International*.

Stage versus Screen

Daniel had to perform in eight shows a week while doing *Equus* onstage, but said his work in the theater was not more difficult than what he had encountered in movies. "There can be really long hours, and you might do 20 takes on any given shot," he said.

Quoted in Elysa Gardner, "Radcliffe Puts the Spurs to His Role in *Equus*," *USA Today*, September 25, 2008.

The movie successfully portrays the pain a family suffers when a young man is sent to war, and Daniel gives a stirring performance as he shows the ordeal Jack endured. "If the role hadn't required him to wear wire rimmed spectacles and an expression of saintly forbearance, I wouldn't have thought of Harry Potter once," said writer Lynsey Hanley on the *New Statesman* Web site. "Heartbreakingly, in the trench scenes he looked like a child dressed as a man, too slight and too sweet to lead men to their deaths."[87] In *Variety* magazine, reviewer Brian Lowry agreed that Daniel successfully took on his new role and added that the movie was a sign that Daniel would enjoy an acting career after the Harry Potter series ended.

The Sixth Potter Film

After portraying a real-life character in *My Boy Jack*, Daniel returned to his role as the fictional Harry Potter for the sixth movie in the series. *Harry Potter and the Half-Blood Prince* again addressed a dark and serious theme, as Harry must deal with an ailing Professor Dumbledore and more threats from Lord Voldemort. The acting experience Daniel gained between the fifth and sixth movies helped him with his portrayal of the young wizard who has a great deal to contend with.

In* Half-Blood Prince, *Harry is determined to destroy Lord Voldemort, the evil wizard responsible for his parents' deaths.

The plot of *Half-Blood Prince* has Harry finding a potions book that is the property of the "Half-Blood Prince." He gathers valuable information from it as he tries to find out the identity of the book's former owner. While he is working through this mystery, his distrust and dislike of Draco Malfoy grows as he suspects Malfoy has evil intentions. He and his friends also try to determine how to destroy Lord Voldemort. "Until now, there's been all sorts of talk about finding and fighting Voldemort," Daniel said. "In this film, Harry starts taking steps towards actually doing that."[88]

The plot of *Half-Blood Prince* also had a lighter side, as Harry and his friends cope with boyfriend and girlfriend issues. Harry realizes he is attracted to Ron's sister, Ginny, but finds it difficult to express his feelings because Ron feels protective toward her. Ron also has a girlfriend, to Hermoine's dismay. For the romantic scenes, director David Yates allowed Daniel and the others to do some improvising rather than give them a scripted scene. The fact that he trusted them to pull off the scene in character showed that they had all grown as actors.

Filming for *Half-Blood Prince* wrapped up in spring 2008. Its release date was delayed until the summer of 2009, in order to give the movie studio a good chance at having a blockbuster movie that season. Plans are to make the seventh Potter book, *Harry Potter and the Deathly Hallows*, into two movies, set for release in 2010 and 2011.

No Regrets about Harry

Although Daniel spent much of his childhood and teen years on the sets of the Harry Potter movies and other films and onstage, he did not feel he had missed out on anything by devoting so much of his time to acting. His life was a happy one, he said, and when he was unhappy, his feelings had more to do with teen insecurity than his work on the movie set. "For the most part I've been happy every single day," he said. "And all the times I've been unhappy, it's never been anything to do with Potter."[89]

As a teen millionaire, critics were worried that Radcliffe would start to behave irresponsibly; however, he has kept a quiet life preferring poetry over nightclubs.

Having a steady acting role meant that Daniel was not around people his own age as often as a typical teenager is, and this made him grow up more quickly. Although there were other children on the set of the Potter movies and other films, he spent much of his time working with adults. This gave him a grown-up way of looking at things. He had friends, but he had to be careful. It was hard to know if a person wanted to be his friend just because he was in the Harry Potter films. Some people who claimed to be friends with Daniel were sometimes not true friends at all and would leak details about his personal life to a tabloid newspaper or post a video of him on YouTube.

Exercise and Junk Food

Daniel jogs and works out to keep his body toned and muscular, but that does not mean that he always eats healthy foods. With a physically demanding role in *Equus* as well as his workouts meant that he could eat junk food without ruining his physique. "He loves Mars bars," said Joanna Christie, who was in the London version of *Equus*. "I don't think he cut down on those at all."

Quoted in Michelle Tauber, "Daniel Radcliffe Grows Up," *People Weekly*, October 6, 2008, p. 93.

In addition to dealing with being famous, Daniel also had to carefully manage his money. He had made millions from the Harry Potter movies, but he was not tempted to spend it recklessly or become self-indulgent. People expected him to do something irresponsible or wild, he says, but that is not who he is. Rather than go out to nightclubs and drink and risk having his picture plastered all over the tabloid newspapers the next day, he prefers to follow his other interests. "I write poetry and I love it," said Daniel, who enjoys reading the poems of John Keats and others. "I like being different from most other people in my generation."[90]

Daniel is careful not to do things that might result in an unflattering news story or photo being printed, but when rumor-filled sensational stories are printed about him, he takes it in stride. He realizes that it is something that comes along with his fame. He tries hard not to give the tabloid press much to write about him, by staying away from nightclubs. When he left the London theater each night after acting in *Equus*, he would wear the same outfit to make the photos of him less valuable. "It's that they're annoyed that I'm growing up adjusted," he said. "They'd much rather I was growing up and going wild and crashing cars."[91]

Nothing Serious

Newspaper articles and photos linked Daniel to several girls but his busy schedule keeps him from having a serious relationship. In 2007 he dated Laura O'Toole, who had been an understudy in *Equus*, and when he was younger, there were rumors that he was dating a twenty-three-year-old hairdresser. However, he said this is not the right time for him to have a steady girlfriend. "Most of my friends have been girls, and I see how they are with their boyfriends, and I think, 'I couldn't do that,'" he said. "I just don't have the time."

Quoted in Michelle Tauber, "Daniel Radcliffe Grows Up," *People Weekly*, October 6, 2008, p. 93.

Equus on Broadway

Daniel was confident in the choices he was making in his life, both in his private life and in his career. He saw no reason to try to impress or shock people by doing something wild in his personal life, and in his professional life he was careful to make solid choices. He did not have to take parts for the amount of money he would be paid, so he chose roles that would help him learn and grow as an actor.

The positive reviews he received for *Equus* strengthened Daniel's confidence in his ability as an actor. At first, some people thought he got the role only because his name brought attention to the play. He had proved them wrong by delivering a strong performance.

Daniel's performance in *Equus* had been so popular in London that the play came to Broadway in 2008. He was thrilled to have the opportunity to act in New York City and received a warm welcome when he arrived. His parents came to New York with him and Racdliffe loved the city and the reception he received.

As usual, Daniel was determined not to be seen as a spoiled child star. He worked diligently and set his ego aside. As a result, his costars enjoyed having him around and found him easy to work with. "He's great, absolutely great,"[92] commented Adesola Osakalumi, who played one of the horses.

Always looking to improve, Daniel wanted to bring something new to the role when he came to the United States. Although he had received positive reviews for his work onstage in London, some reviewers had commented that he did not project his voice as well as a seasoned stage actor did. Daniel worked to correct this and also looked to bring more depth to the role of Alan Strang. To help him better understand the themes of the play, he watched the 1971 movie *A Clockwork Orange*. The movie talks about taking away a person's individuality and has some themes that are similar to those in *Equus*. Watching the movie and doing acting exercises, such as imagining different areas of a room representing different emotions, helped Daniel bring stronger feelings to the role. "I didn't want to just rehash the performance," Daniel explained. "I wanted it to be a lot stronger and have a lot more anger."[93]

Cheers for Daniel

When *Equus* premiered on Broadway in September 2008, Daniel again received positive reviews for his work. Critic Elysa Gardner noted that he was clearly ready for adult roles, while *New York* Times critic Ben Brantley said, "The young wizard has chosen wisely."[94] He said that Daniel fit nicely into the role, and grabbed the audience's attention by the way he used his eyes.

As the critics in London had commented, the play itself seemed dated in its views and themes. However, Daniel rose above the material. In *Variety*, David Rooney said that Daniel made an "impressive debut"[95] and that his performance made up for the stale theme of the play, noting that, "Radcliffe's performance provides the play with a raw emotional nerve center."[96]

As in London, Daniel's performance helped audiences in the United States realize that he was a young actor, not to be confused with a young wizard. "You might not know it from watching him play a boy wizard in the seemingly endless Harry Potter film franchise, but Daniel Radcliffe has grown into his own as an actor,"

Radcliffe was cast in a movie to portray British photo – journalist Dan Eldon who was killed in Somalia in 1993.

said reviewer Thom Geier, noting that he brought a "high-strung vulnerability to the role of Alan Strang." [97]

The positive comments he heard about his role in *Equus*, gave Daniel a good feeling about his future. He saw himself taking on many acting opportunities. "I hope to play as many characters as I can," he said. "I'll keep coming back to the stage and film for as long as they'll have me." [98]

A New Chapter Begins

Daniel performed in *Equus* through February 2009, and then moved on to the final Potter movies. He was also cast as British photojournalist Dan Eldon in a movie about Eldon's life. Eldon was murdered at the age of twenty-two in Somalia in 1993. By taking on challenging and varied roles such as Jack Kipling and Alan Strang, Daniel had set himself up for more interesting parts and a solid career.

Daniel's life as Harry Potter will wrap up when he is twenty-one. When Daniele looks toward the end of the movie series, he feels both sad and intrigued. It will be difficult to leave behind the people he has enjoyed working with over the years, but it will be interesting to move on to new things. "That will have been 10 years of my life and that's a huge chunk," he noted. "So I'll be sad because it will be the end of an era in a way. But I equally imagine it will be quite exciting to be out of that world." [99] In an interview with *Details* magazine, he took an optimistic and eager view of his future and summed it up this way: "I can't wait." [100]

Chapter 1: A Child Eager to Act

1. Quoted in Sharon Churcher, "Harry Potter: The Brain Disorder which Means I Can't Tie My Shoelaces," Mail Online, August 16, 2008, http://dailymail.co.uk/tvshowbiz/article-1046031.
2. Celia Wren, "Dickens on the Tube," *Commonweal*, April 7, 2000, p. 21.
3. Terry Kelleher, "Picks and Pans Main: Tube," *People*, April 17, 2000, p. 27.
4. Roger Ebert, "The Tailor of Panama," rogerebert.com, March 30, 2001, http://rogerebert.suntimes.com/apps/pbcs.dll/article?AID=/20010330/REVIEWS/103300303/1023.
5. Quoted in Jess Cagle, "The First Look at Harry Potter," *Time*, November 5, 2001, p. 88.
6. Quoted in Barry Koltnow, "One Enchanted Night at the Theater, Radcliffe became Harry Potter," EastValleyTribune.com, July 6, 2007, www.eastvalleytribune.com/story/92834?source=rss&dest=STY-92834.
7. Quoted in Andrew Pincus et al., "Ones to Watch," *Hollywood Reporter–International*, November 2000, p. 36.
8. Quoted in *Newsweek*, "International Perspectives," *Newsweek*, September 4, 2000, p. 19.
9. Quoted in Dana Harris "'Potter' Waves Wand over Brit," *Variety*, August 28, 2000, p. 10.
10. Quoted in Daniel Fierman, "Casting a Spell," *Entertainment Weekly*, September 1, 2000, p. 16.
11. Quoted in Jeff Jensen and Daniel Fierman, "Inside Harry Potter," *Entertainment Weekly*, September 14, 2001, www.ew.com/ew/article/0,,254808,00.html.

Chapter 2: Bringing Harry Potter to Life

12. Quoted in *Hollywood Reporter–International*, "Chris Columbus," *Hollywood Reporter–International*, November 20, 2001, p. S-4.

13. Quoted in Jane Sanderson, "Harry Potter and the Philosopher's Stone," *Tribute*, November 2001, p. 22.
14. Quoted in Cagle, "The First Look at Harry Potter," p. 88.
15. Quoted in Christine Spines, "Harry Potter and the Sorcerer's Stone," *National Geographic World*, November 2001, p. 12.
16 Quoted in *Scholastic News*, "Talking Teamwork," *Scholastic News*, October 1, 2001, p. 2.
17. Quoted in Jensen and Fierman, "Inside Harry Potter."
18. Quoted in *People*, "Leapin' Wizards!" *People*, November 19, 2001, p. 64.
19. Quoted in Tim Robey, "London Greets 'Harry,'" *Daily Variety*, November 6, 2001, p. 4.
20. Lisa Schwarzbaum, "Hogwarts and All: The World's Favorite Boy Wizard Pulls off a Predictable Magic Trick in *Harry Potter and the Sorcerer's Stone*," *Entertainment Weekly*, November 23, 2001, p. 52.
21. Leah Rozen, "Picks and Pans: Screen," *People*, November 25, 2001, p. 39.
22. Stanley Kauffmann, "Wizard of Two Kinds," *New Republic*, December 10, 2001, p. 24.
23. Schwarzbaum, "Hogwarts and All," p. 52.
24. Quoted in Claudia Puig, "A Potion for Potter Success," *USA Today*, November 15, 2002.
25. Quoted in *People*, "Pop Quiz with Daniel Radcliffe," *People*, November 11, 2002, p. 24.
26. Quoted in Puig, "A Potion for Potter Success."
27. Quoted in Simon Garfield, "Daniel Radcliffe," *Details*, http://men.style.com/details/features/landing?id=content_5746.
28. Quoted in *USA Today*, "Secret's Out: Girls Love Harry Potter," *USA Today*, November 4, 2002.
29. Mike Clark, "Potter Pure Magic This Time," *USA Today*, November 15, 2002.
30. Lisa Schwarzbaum, "Spell Check," *Entertainment Weekly*, November 22, 2002, p. 49.
31. Quoted in *Evening Standard*, "It's Harry the Teenage Wizard," *Evening Standard*, June 3, 2003.

Chapter 3: Daniel and Harry Grow Up

32. Quoted in Daniel Fierman, "Harry Potter and the Challenge of Sequels," *Entertainment Weekly*, November 22, 2002, p. 24.
33. Quoted in Jeff Jensen, "Lucky Thirteen?" *Entertainment Weekly*, June 11, 2004, p. 32.
34. Quoted in Jensen, "Lucky Thirteen?" p. 32.
35. Ty Burr, "Magic Carpet Ride," *Entertainment Weekly*, November 26, 2004, p. 98.
36. Leah Rozen, "Harry Potter and the Prisoner of Azkaban," *People*, June 14, 2004, p. 31.
37. Steve Vineberg, "Wizard Comes of Age," *Christian Century*, June 29, 2004, p. 42.
38. Sean Smith, "Lightning Strikes," *Newsweek*, May 31, 2004, p. 64.
39. Quoted in *Time for Kids*, "TFK Q&A," *Time for Kids*, May 7, 2004, p. 8.
40. Quoted in Lev Grossman and Jumana Farouky, "Growing Up Potter," *Time*, December 5, 2005, p. 60.
41. Quoted in *People*, "Hogwarts 2004," *People*, June 14, 2004, p. 126.
42. Quoted in Grossman and Farouky, "Growing Up Potter," p. 60.
43. Quoted in Jeff Jensen, "Daniel Radcliffe," *Entertainment Weekly*, November 11, 2005, p. 26.
44. Quoted in Jensen, "Daniel Radcliffe," p. 26.
45. Shirley Sealy, "Harry Potter and the Goblet of Fire," *Film Journal International*, December 2005, p. 61.
46. Peter Travers, "Harry Potter and the Goblet of Fire," *Rolling Stone*, December 1, 2005, p. 136.
47. Owen Gleiberman, "Harry Potter and the Goblet of Fire," *Entertainment Weekly*, November 25, 2005, p. 76.
48. *People*, "Harry Potter and the Goblet of Fire," *People*, November 28, 2005, p. 48.
49. Quoted in Jeff Jensen, "Harry Potter," *Entertainment Weekly*, December 30, 2005, p. 60.
50. Quoted in Jensen, "Daniel Radcliffe," p. 26.

Chapter 4: A Career beyond Harry

51. Quoted in Steve Daly, "Harry Potter and the Grown-Up Drama," *Entertainment Weekly*, www.ew.com/ew/article/0,,20057083,00.html.
52. Quoted in Daly, "Harry Potter and the Grown-Up Drama."
53. Quoted in Daly, "Harry Potter and the Grown-Up Drama."
54. David Noh, "December Boys," *Film Journal International*, October 2007, p. 56.
55. Noh, "December Boys," p. 56.
56. Quoted in Borys Kit, "'Potter' Takes the Fifth," *Hollywood Reporter–International*, July 10, 2007, p. 16.
57. Quoted in Steve Daly, "Harry the 5th," *Entertainment Weekly*, July 20, 2007, p. 30.
58. Quoted in Sean Smith, "Who's That Guy with Harry Potter?" *Newsweek*, December 18, 2006, p. 22.
59. Quoted in Smith, "Who's That Guy with Harry Potter?" p. 22.
60. Quoted in Daly, "Harry the 5th," p. 30.
61. Quoted in Daly, "Harry the 5th," p. 30.
62. Quoted in Mike Goodridge, "Harry's Welcome Back to World," *Evening Standard*, May 31, 2007.
63. Quoted in Claudia Puig, "Dark Magic Haunts Hogwarts," *USA Today*, July 10, 2007.
64. Quoted in Goodridge, "Harry's Welcome Back to World."
65. Quoted in Puig, "Dark Magic Haunts Hogwarts."
66. Quoted in Daly, "Harry the 5th," p. 30.
67. Quoted in Daly, "Harry the 5th," p. 30.

Chapter 5: Conquering the Stage

68. Quoted in Sarah Lyall, "Onstage, Stripped of That Wizardry," *New York Times*, September 14, 2008.
69. Quoted in David Benedict, "Blinded by the Light," *Variety*, February 26, 2007, p. 39.
70. Quoted in Benedict, "Blinded by the Light," p. 39.
71. Quoted in Benedict, "Blinded by the Light," p. 39.
72. Quoted in Jasper Rees, "A Demanding Kind of Horse Play," Telegraph.co.uk, February 26, 2007,

www.telegraph.co.uk/arts/main.jhtml?xml=/arts/2007/02/26/btequus26.xml.

73. Quoted in Steve Daly, "Harry Potter and the Grown-Up Drama," *Entertainment Weekly*, www.ew.com/ew/article/0,,20051365_20057083,00.html..
74. Matt Wolf, "Horse Play," *Entertainment Weekly*, March 16, 2007, p. 77.
75. Quoted in Rebecca Winters Keegan, "Q&A Michael Gambon," *Time*, March 5, 2007, p. 79.
76. Quoted in Daly, "Harry the 5th," p. 30.
77. David Ansen, "A Not Very Scary Harry," *Newsweek*, July 23, 2007, p. 51.
78. Leah Rozen, "Harry Potter and the Order of the Phoenix," *People*, July 23, 2007, p. 35.
79. Rozen, "Harry Potter and the Order of the Phoenix," p. 35.
80. Richard Corliss, "I Was a Teenage Wizard," *Time*, July 16, 2007, p. 66.
81. Quoted in Steve Daly, "Phoenix Rising," *Entertainment Weekly*, April 6, 2007, p. 24.
82. Quoted in *USA Today*, "Daniel Radcliffe, Torn between Two Worlds," *USA Today*, July 10, 2007.
83. Quoted in *USA Today*, "Daniel Radcliffe, Torn between Two Worlds."

Chapter 6: Ready for Adult Roles

84. Quoted in Sam Richards, "Soldier of Fortune," Telegraph.co.uk, October 11, 2007, www.telegraph.co.uk/arts/main.jhtml?xml=/arts/2007/11/10/nosplit/bvtvsaturday10.xml.
85. Quoted in Richards, "Soldier of Fortune."
86. Laurence Vittes, "My Boy Jack," *Hollywood Reporter–International*, April 18, 2008, p. 15.
87. Lynsey Hanley, "Because Our Fathers Lied," *New Statesman*, November 15, 1997, www.newstatesman.com/television/2007/11/kipling-haig-son-john-war-itv1.
88. Jeff Jensen, "There Will Be Half-Blood," *People*, http://www.ew.com/ew/article/0,,20218889,00.html.

89. Quoted in Chris Norris, "Daniel Radcliffe," *Details*, September 8, 2008, http://men.style.com/details/blogs/thegadabout/2008/09/daniel-radcliff.html.
90. Quoted in Norris, "Daniel Radcliffe."
91. Quoted in Simon Garfield, "Daniel Radcliffe," *Details*, http://men.style.com/details/features/landing?id=content_5746.
92. Quoted in Jessica Gold Haralson, "Daniel Radcliffe; I Love Broadway!" *People*, September 7, 2008, www.people.com/people/article/0,,20224061,00.html?xid=rss-fullcontent.
93. Quoted in Lyall, "Onstage, Stripped of That Wizardry."
94. Ben Brantley, "In the Darkness of the Stable," *New York Times*, September 26, 2008.
95. David Rooney, "Radcliffe Gives Shaky Horseplay Fresh Kick," *Variety*, September 29, 2008, p. 57.
96. Rooney, "Radcliffe Gives Shaky Horseplay Fresh Kick," p. 57.
97. Thom Geier, "Equus," *Entertainment Weekly*, October 3, 2008, p. 83.
98. Quoted in Elysa Gardner, "Radcliffe Puts the Spurs to His Role in *Equus*," *USA Today*, September 25, 2008.
99. Quoted in John Hiscock, "How Harry Potter and Friends Grew Up," Telegraph.co.uk, June 29, 2007, www.telegraph.co.uk/arts/main.jhtml?xml=/arts/2007/06/29/nosplit/bfpotter129.xml.
100. Quoted in Norris, "Daniel Radcliffe."

Important Dates

1989

Daniel Jacob Radcliffe is born on July 23 to Alan Radcliffe and Marcia Gresham.

1999

Daniel is cast in *David Copperfield*, playing Copperfield as a young boy.

2000

Daniel gets a small role in *The Tailor of Panama*, and the lead role in *Harry Potter and the Sorcerer's Stone*.

2001

Harry Potter and the Sorcerer's Stone is released and becomes the top movie of the year.

2002

Harry Potter and the Chamber of Secrets is released.

2004

Harry Potter and the Prisoner of Azkaban is released.

2005

Harry Potter and the Goblet of Fire is released; Daniel films the movie *December Boys*.

2007

Harry Potter and the Order of the Phoenix, *My Boy Jack*, and *December Boys* are released. Daniel appears onstage in London in *Equus*.

2008

Harry Potter and the Half-Blood Prince, is filmed. *Equus* moves to Broadway.

2009

Harry Potter and the Half-Blood Prince is scheduled for release in July.

For More Information

Books

John Bankston, *Daniel Radcliffe*. Hockessin, DE: Mitchell Lane, 2004. This easy-to-read biography tells how Daniel got the lead role in *Harry Potter and the Sorcerer's Stone* and discusses the impact the role has had on his life.

Grace Norwich, *Daniel Radcliffe: No Ordinary Wizard*. New York: Simon Spotlight, 2008. This biography of Daniel includes information on his first work in show business and his work on the Harry Potter movies. It also includes pages of colorful photographs.

Stephanie Watson, *Daniel Radcliffe: Film and Stage Star*. Berkeley Heights, NJ: Enslow, 2009. This biography of Daniel Radcliffe looks at his life as a popular celebrity.

Periodical

Michelle Tauber, "Daniel Radcliffe Grows Up," *People Weekly*, October 6, 2008.

Web Sites

DanRadcliffe.com (www.danradcliffe.com). This is a fan Web site devoted to Daniel Radcliffe. It includes video clips, photos, and news items related to the actor.

Internet Movie Database (www.imdb.com). This Web site offers detailed information about movies, including casts, crews, reviews, and trivia. A brief biography of Daniel Radcliffe and an updated list of his film work is available here.

Warner Bros. Studios (www.harrypotter.warnerbros.com). This is the official site of the Harry Potter movies.

Index

Picture Credits

Cover: © Phil McCarten/Reuters/Corbis
AFFC/Village Roadshow Pictures/The Kobal Collection, 56, 58
Alan Davidson/WireImage/Getty Images, 45
Alberto E. Rodriguez/Getty Images, 63
Amanda Edwards/Getty Images, 39
Andrew H. Walker/Getty Images, 53
AP Images, 9, 19, 31, 36, 69, 90
Bruce Glikas/FilmMagic/Getty Images, 70
Chris Jackson/Getty Images, 78
David Cheskin/EPA/Landov, 21
Eamonn McCormack/WireImage/Getty Images, 73
Eric Charbonneau/WireImage/Getty Images, 75, 84
Evan Agostini/Image Direct/Getty Images, 13
Jo Hale/Getty Images, 48
Ken Goff Photos/WireImage/Getty Images, 43
© Peter Brown/Alamy, 81
Peter Mountain/WireImage/Getty Images, 25
© Photos 12/Alamy, 33, 51
Sylvia Linares/FilmMagic/Getty Images, 86
© Trinity Mirror/Mirrorpix/Alamy, 29
Urbano Delvalle/Time Life Pictures/Getty Images, 26
© Warner Bros/ Courtesy Everett Collection, 60, 65
© WGBH/Courtesy Everett Collection, 16

About the Author

Terri Dougherty loves writing biographies that kids like to read. She has written dozens of books for children and lives in Appleton, Wisconsin, with her husband, Denis, and their three children, Kyle, Rachel, and Emily. They enjoy the Harry Potter books and see each new Harry Potter movie as soon as they can.